The Teaching Power of Dreams

Using Your Dreams to Change Your Life

Sherry and Brad Steiger

1469 Morstein Road
West Chester, Pennsylvania 19380 U.S.A.

The Teaching Power of Dreams: Using Your Dreams
to Change Your Life

by Sherry and Brad Steiger

Library of Congress Card Number: 89-052097
International Standard Book Number: 0-924608-04-8

Manufactured in the United States of America

Published by Whitford Press,
A division of
Schiffer Publishing, Ltd.
1469 Morstein Road
West Chester, Pennsylvania 19380
Please write for a free catalog.
This book may be purchased from the publisher.
Please include $2.00 postage.
Try your bookstore first.

Contents

Chapter 1

Good Dream Time Is Essential to Good Health

Evolving humankind has always been fascinated by its dreams. Whether these sleep time adventures were considered voyages of the soul, messages from the gods, the doorway of the unconscious or accidental by-products of insufficient oxygen in the brain, thoughtful men and women have sought to learn more about this intriguing, kaleidoscopic activity of the sleeping consciousness.

It is important to note immediately in a book about the receiving of dream teachings that throughout history the process of interpreting dreams has been held in very high esteem.

For example, the Talmud, the Hebrew sacred book of practical wisdom, tells us very clearly that the Jews gave great importance both to the dream and to the dream interpreter. "An uninterpreted dream is like an unopened letter," wrote Rabbi Hisda.

The whole religion of Islam is based on the great initiatory dream of Mohammed. The Prophet relied heavily on his dreams and on those of his followers. Each morning he called his disciples together to discuss their dreams and to formulate his ongoing teachings.

Among the ancients there were the dream incubation temples of Serapis, Egyptian god of dreams; and later, of Aesculapius, the Greek god of healing. Thousands of people made their pilgrimage to seek advice and healing. After rigorous periods of fasting, prayer, and sacred ritual, they might sleep in the temple and receive their longed-for dream.

Plato saw dreams as a release for passionate inner forces; Aristotle debunked the idea of dreams being of divine origin.

In the second century, another Greek, Artemidorous of Ephesus, produced the *Oneirocritica*, the encyclopedia that was the forerunner to thousands of dream books throughout the ages.

During the late Middle Ages, dreams were sometimes feared by Christians to be a door to evil. Dreams began to fall into disfavor in spite of the fact that throughout the Bible the idea of God speaking directly to man through dreams and visions is commonplace.

> *Genesis 28:12*: Jacob had a dream of a ladder set up on earth, the top of it reaching to heaven. He beheld in this dream angels of God ascending and descending on the ladder with the Lord standing above it confirming the covenant of Abraham to Jacob.

> *Job 33:14*: "For God speaketh once, yea twice, yet a man perceiveth it not.
>
> "In a dream, in a vision of the night, when sleep falleth upon men in slumberings upon the bed; then He openeth the ears of men, and speaketh their instructions, that he may withdraw man from his purpose and hide pride from man."

Edgar Cayce, America's most famous clairvoyant, often referred to as the Sleeping Prophet, stated: "Any condition ever becoming reality is *first dreamed*." Perhaps this is so, and it is "hidden" in dreams by a wise Creator for the reasons given in Job 33:14. It requires work and sincerity on our part to "listen" and "interpret."

Again, in the Old Testament, *Jeremiah 23:28* states: "The prophet that hath a dream, let him tell a dream, and he that hath My word, let him speak My word faithfully."

Daniel 2:6: "Show me the dream and the interpretation thereof."

Daniel 2:28: "There is a God in heaven that revealeth secrets!"

Joel 2:28: "Your old men shall dream dreams, your young men shall see visions."

Dreams, or "night visions," might be auditory and present a direct message (as in *Job 33:15-17, Genesis 20:3,6*) or at other times be symbolic, requiring skilled interpretation. The Mesopotamian and Egyptian courts employed skilled professionals who sought to interpret dreams and visions (*Genesis 41:8; Daniel 2:2*).

Books were compiled in which various dream phenomena and their implications were recorded for reference purposes.

The Israelites, by contrast, believed that interpretation of dreams could be accomplished *only* with Yahweh's guidance (*Genesis 40:8*). Joseph and Daniel were two Israelites who attained high regard for their skill as dream interpreters. In *Daniel 7:16*, Daniel required the help of an angel to interpret a complex dream.

Mosaic Law prescribed the death penalty for false interpreters who, claiming to know God's will, were eager for a sign or a wonder to support their assertions.

The prophets Jeremiah and Zechariah warned against such pseudodreamers, as well as those who gave false consolation or introduced the worship of other gods, such as Baal.

Because of the revelatory value of dreams (*Numbers 12:6*) individuals frequently attempted to *induce* such visions through the incubation process of spending the night in a temple or holy place. This practice was commonly employed by the cultic prophets of Mari and the kings of Lagash and Ugarit. King Solomon received both *wisdom* and *warning* in dreams (*1 Kings 3:5, 9:2*).

The New Testament accounts surrounding the birth of Jesus record a number of revelatory dreams. Joseph was instructed to wed Mary and was assured of her purity (*Matthew 1:20*), in spite of the apparent fact that she was already pregnant. Joseph, in despair and humiliation of violating the strictures of his religion, must have had a *very* convincing dream. Later, Joseph was warned to flee to Egypt (*Matthew 2:13*), return (verse 19) and to go to Galilee (verse 22).

The Magi (the three wise men) were warned in a dream not to return to their native land along the same route as they had come (verses 2, 12) because of Herod's evil intentions.

In *Acts 2:17* we read the prophetic verse: "And it shall come to pass in the last days saith God, I will pour out of my spirit upon all flesh; and your sons and daughters shall prophesy [preach) and your young men shall see visions, and your old men shall dream dreams."

By the late-nineteenth century dreams were being examined

from a physiological perspective. The ancient notion that God spoke directly to men in dreams was pretty much dismissed. Then came the groundbreaking work of Sigmund Freud and Carl Jung.

In 1899, Sigmund Freud, a Viennese psychiatrist and the founder of psychoanalysis, brought dreams into the realm of the scientific community. Freud's theory was basically that the dream was a disguised wish fulfillment of infantile sexual needs, which were repressed by built-in censors of the waking mind. The apparent content of the dream was only concealing a shockingly latent dream.

Through the use of a complex process of "dream work," which Freud developed, the dream could be unraveled backward, penetrating the unconscious memory of the dreamer and thereby setting the person free.

Swiss psychiatrist Carl G. Jung, a student and later dissenter of Freud, added new dimensions to the understanding of the Self through dreams. "Sigmund Freud confirmed for most people the existing contempt for the psyche," Jung wrote. "It had been merely overlooked and neglected; now it had become a dump for moral refuse. The discovery that the unconscious is no mere depository of the past, but it is also full of germs of future psychic situations and ideas, led me to my own new approach to psychology."

Jung saw the dream as a compensatory mechanism whose function was to restore one's psychological balance. His collective unconscious linked man with his ancestors as part of the evolutionary tendency of the human mind. Jung found startling similarities in the unconscious contents and the symbolic processes of both modern and primitive humans.

He recognized archetypes: "Mental forces whose presence cannot be explained by anything in the individual's own life, but seemed to be aboriginal, innate and inherited shapes of the human mind."

Jung's theory is that it is crucial to pay attention to the archetypes met in dream life. Of special importance is the *shadow*, a figure of the same sex as the dreamer, which contains all the repressed characteristics one has not developed in his conscious life. The *anima* is the personification of all the female tendencies, both positive and negative, in the male psyche. Its counterpart in the female psyche is the *animus*.

The most mysterious but most significant of the Jungian archetypes is the *Self*, which M. L. von Fram describes in *Man and
His Symbols* as the regulating center that brings about a constant
expansion and maturing of the personality, "...and the fulfillment
of that process... the 'Cosmic Man' who lives within the heart
of every individual, and yet at the same time fills the entire cosmos."

The Self emerges only when the ego can surrender and merge
into it. (Jung saw the self as encompassing the *total* psyche, of
which the ego is only a small part.) Jung called this psychic
integration of the personality, this striving toward wholeness, the
process of "individuation."

Jung rejected arbitrary interpretations of dreams and dismissed
free Freudian association as "wandering too far from the dream
content." Jung developed an intricate system of "elaborations,"
in which the dreamer relates all that he knows about a symbol-
-as if he were explaining it to a visitor from another planet.

A New Era of Dream Research

Most authorities would probably consider Dr. Nathaniel Kleitman
to be the father of modern scientific dream research, for he pursued
the subject when his colleagues dismissed the area as having no
value. As a professor of philosophy at the University of Chicago,
Dr. Kleitman asked a graduate student, Eugene Aserinsky, to study
the relationship of eye movement and sleep.

In 1951 Aserinsky identified rapid eye movement (REM) and
demonstrated that the brain is active during sleep, thus establishing
the course for other dream researchers to follow.

Although discussions of REM are now commonplace in the
conversations of informed laypeople, it should be noted that prior
to the work of Kleitman and Aserinsky most scientists maintained
that the brain "tuned down" during sleep.

Today there are at least 170 sleep clinics operating in the United
States, and their analyses cite over 50 sleep disorders. A kind
of general consensus of these scientists expresses the opinion that-
-second only to the common cold--sleep disorders constitute the
most common health complaint.

These researchers also have noted a mysterious kinship between mental illness and sleep--and even longevity and sleep.

If you take due note of the above findings, it should become increasingly obvious that our insistence that you learn to understand your dreams and use them in the most productive way possible can only help to bring about a healthy union of body, mind, and spirit.

A Good Night's Sleep

Pursuing the REM research, Dr. Kleitman and another of his medical students, William C. Dement, found what may be the pattern for a "good night's sleep."

They discovered that there appears to be a nightly pattern of sleep that begins with about 90 minutes of non-REM rest during which our brainwaves gradually lengthen and progress through four distinct stages of sleep, with Stage Four the deepest stage. It is then that the first REM episode of the night begins.

Rapid eye movement is now observable, but the body itself remains still. The central nervous system becomes extremely active during REM. It becomes so intensely active that Dr. Frederick Snyder, of the National Institute of Mental Health (NIMH), termed the activity "a third state of earthly existence," distinct from both non-REM sleep and wakefulness.

The breathing is even in non-REM sleep. During the REM episode breathing may accelerate to a panting pace. The rhythm of the heart may speed up or slow down unaccountably. Blood pressure can dramatically fall. Usually a penile (male) or clitoral (female) engorgement accompanies these REM intervals.

According to Dr. Snyder, "The same enlivenment takes place in vital functions throughout the body. Metabolism rises. The kidneys make less, but more concentrated urine. Spontaneous firing of nerve cells in many brain regions is increased *beyond* the level of waking."

Other physiological changes also occur during REM. The flow of blood to our brains increases about 40 percent. Then we stir and return to the non-REM sleep cycle. This pattern repeats itself throughout the night.

"Man in His Dreams Becomes a Creator"

Psychologists Montague Ullman, Joseph Adelson, Howard Shevrin, and Frederick Weiss have done much to advance the thesis that dreams basically are creative. This concept of the dream as a creative tool may be somewhat alien to Western thought, but numerous Eastern writings, including the ancient Hindu *Upanishads*, speak of this aspect of the dream. One of the *Upanishads* tells us that "...Man in his dreams becomes a creator. There are no real chariots in that state...no blessings...no joys, but he himself creates blessings, happiness and joys."

Dr. Stanley Krippner, former director of the Dream Laboratory at Maimonides Hospital in Brooklyn, New York, maintains that the principal function of the dream is a biological one. Dr. Krippner sees some dreams as meaningful while others may be insignificant bits of mental fluff.

Dreaming, in Dr. Krippner's estimation, is a primary means of brain development and maturation. Newborn infants spend about half of their sleeping time in the rapid-eye-movement (REM) or dream state. Although such dreams probably are concerned with tactile impressions rather than memories, Dr. Krippner believes that these dreams "...probably prepare the infants' immature nervous systems for the onslaught of experience coming with the maturation of vision, hearing and the other senses."

To further support this theory, Dr. Krippner cites studies done with older subjects that indicate that young adults spend 25 percent of their time dreaming while the proportion decreases to 20 percent among the elderly. It seems that the brain, once it is functioning well, does not need as much dream time.

Dr. Carlyle Smith and his colleagues at Trent University in Ontario found that REM sleep is crucial to the learning of new skills. "REM sleep," he states, "is somehow involved in developing or processing new mental strategies."

The Brain Must Stay "In Tune"

Recent experiments demonstrate that simple forms of mental functioning go on at night even when the individual is not dreaming. The brain appears to require constant stimulation even during sleep and may use dream periods to "keep in tune" and to process information that has accumulated during the day.

Dr. Krippner does not argue with the theory that dreaming represents a means by which a sleeper expresses his wishes and works out his tensions, but he holds that such dream functions are secondary to the development and informational tasks of dreaming.

The Importance of Dream Sleep

How important is dream sleep?

In the mid-1950s Drs. William Dement and Charles Fischer, working at Mount Sinai Hospital in New York, decided to find out. Volunteers were asked to spend several nights in the laboratory. They were awakened throughout the night each time the electro-encephalograph indicated the start of a dream period. These volunteers got all of their regular sleep *except* for their dream time. After five nights of dreamlessness, they became nervous, jittery, irritable and had trouble concentrating. One volunteer quit the project in a panic.

Another group of volunteers in another part of the hospital were awakened the same number of times each night as those in the first group, but they were awakened when they were *not* dreaming. In other words, they were allowed approximately their usual amount of dream time. These volunteers suffered none of the troubles and upsets that afflicted the first group. This Dement and Fischer experiment presented for the first time evidence that regular dream sleep is essential to physical well-being.

In these experiments some volunteers went as long as 15 nights without dream sleep, at which point they tried to dream all of the time and the researchers had to awaken them constantly. When their dream time was no longer interrupted, the volunteers spent much more time than normal in dream sleep and continued to do so until they had "made up" their dream loss.

When we are deprived of REM sleep, a rebound effect occurs. Dr. William Dement states the situation in very firm words:

If you are not getting your share of REM and non-REM and are feeling sleepy, you are a menace. People who have accumulated a large sleep debt are dangerous on the highway, dangerous in the sky, dangerous wherever they are. That is because an attack of uncontrollable sleepiness is as unpredictable as an earthquake and maybe just as devastating!

Along with other researchers, Dr. Dement believes that sleepiness may in fact have been the true cause of such nuclear disasters as the one at Chernobyl in the Soviet Union and Three Mile Island in the United States. Drowsiness also may have been responsible for the gas leak disaster in Bhopal, India.

Sleep scientists have found that the brain shows significant signs of fatigue even *before* performance begins to lessen, thus suggesting possible methods of forewarning.

The early identification of such symptoms of sleep deprivation could be of benefit to all of us--whether we are driving a car or preparing dinner...whether we are an air-traffic controller or the pilot flying the 747!

Your Life May Depend on Hearing Your Body Clock Ticking

Although it is argued that we may have more than one, we each have at least one "clock" within our bodies. This marvelous mechanism operates on a cycle of about 24 hours and regulates the body's circadian (body) rhythms.

According to Dr. Dement and other researchers, the body rhythms include the timing of hormone releases, variations in blood volume, urine excretions, and most importantly, the oscillations of body temperature that influence the sleep-wakefulness cycle.

Prior to a vital discovery made by Dr. Charles A. Czeisler in 1981, researchers believed that the onset of sleepiness and the amount of time that we sleep primarily were determined by the schedule of our activities preceding sleep. Dr. Czeisler, associate professor of medicine at Harvard Medical School, found that our body clock determines when and how long we will sleep by prompting a temperature decline at night.

The "worst time" for grogginess, according to Dr. Czeisler, is during the body's temperature trough in the latter part of the night. During this period, as many shift workers can attest, sleep seems almost irresistible.

Even ordinary sleepiness can be hazardous. Dr. Torbjorn Akerstedt of the Karolinska Institute in Stockholm noted that when the body clock and the work schedule clash, people can drift in and out of so-called "microsleeps"--without being aware of them!

Dr. Martin Moore-Ede, associate professor of physiology at Harvard and a circadian rhythm specialist, states that such assaults on the body rhythms afflict an estimated 60 million shift workers.

"Most managers are unaware that as many as 80 percent of their workers are nodding off on the night shift," he states. Dr. Moore-Ede has worked with 50 companies worldwide, assisting them revamping their schedules and training their personnel to stay awake.

According to his research findings, even if you have missed just two hours of sleep in one night, you are sleep deprived.

Dr. Czeisler has demonstrated a recent discovery that uses bright lights to shift the body's circadian rhythms, thus enabling an individual to reset his body clock to whatever time he chooses.

Dreams Are as Important as Food and Drink

Dr. Krippner believes that dreaming is as necessary to man as eating and drinking.

> In addition to processing data to keep the brain "in tune" there is also evidence that a biochemical substance that accumulates during the day can only be eliminated from the nervous system during dream periods. One should be as concerned that he receives adequate dream time at night as that he receives adequate food during the day!
>
> Any disturbance that interrupts sleep will interfere with dream time, thus leaving the individual less well pre-pared--physically and psychologically--to face the coming

day. Alcohol, amphetamines and barbiturates depress the amount of dreaming an individual can experience during the night, and users of these drugs should be aware of the fact. Coffee, however, does not seem to depress dream time.

According to studies at the University of California, San Diego, human beings, if left to their own devices, fall into spontaneous daydreams every 90 minutes. It could be that these natural cycles are as necessary to the optimum functioning of the entire body-mind organism as is REM sleep.

Dr. Patricia Carrington, a Princeton University psychologist and an authority on meditation, expresses her hypothesis that humankind is "...starved for the natural rhythms, the biological alternation of rest and relaxation that we see in animals. Only in man is there such a thing as 17 hours of constant wakefulness."

One of the reasons why we use drugs, alcohol, caffeine and other means of altering our states of consciousness may be to somehow manipulate our body-mind structure into obeying the schedule that we have forced upon it--rather than permitting it to follow the natural cycles and rhythms of life itself.

Dr. Jurgen Zulley, psychologist at the Max Planck Institute for Psychiatry in Munich, has found evidence for a four-hour sleep-wake cycle with nap periods at approximately 9:00 A.M., 1:00 P.M., and 5:00 P.M. Dr. Zulley feels that we shouldn't try to combat our natural drowsiness at these times with coffee breaks or with exercise. In his opinion we should seek to be "biologically correct."

It would be better for our health, Dr. Zulley advises, if we took a short nap or just leaned back in our chair for a bit of relaxation rather than reaching for a soft drink or a cup of coffee to keep our mental motors running.

The Role of Environment

Dream researchers also have learned that environment appears to have a marked effect on dreams. One may have unusual dreams when spending the night in a friend's home or in a dream laboratory.

"In our studies at Maimonides," Dr. Krippner observes,

we found that the subjects' dreams often contained references to the electroencephalograph and to the electrodes on their heads, especially during the first night in which they participated in the study. Charles Tart, one of the nation's most eminent sleep and dream researchers, suggests that dream content also will differ with the demands placed upon the dreamer; dreams which are written down at home and given to a researcher will differ from dreams given to a psychotherapist, because in the latter instance the emphasis is on the person's inner life and his attempts to change his behavior.

It has been noted that patients who go to Freudian psychotherapists eventually begin to incorporate Freudian symbols into their dreams while patients who see Jungian analysts do the same with Jungian symbols.

Presleep Experiences

Apparently opinions on the degree to which external events influence dreams vary widely. Some dream researchers contend that all dreams are the result of presleep experiences, while Freudian psychoanalysts emphasize the *internal* determinants of dream content (i.e., one's unconscious drives and defenses).

"The presleep experiences (as part of one's 'day residue') may be used by the unconscious," Dr. Krippner explains, "but they are not of major significance in dream interpretation."

Experimental attempts to determine the accuracy of these two extreme positions dates back to 1889 when Monroe placed cloves on the tongues of several subjects just before they went to bed; three of the 254 reported dreams which involved having cloves on the tongue.

In 1965 Witkin and Lewis reported the soundest experiments to date. Subjects were shown films before retiring and their dreams were collected during the night.

Most subjects dreamed about the films as well as about their personal wishes and problems.

In 1967, Charles Tart presented a list of the various items which influence dreams. Tart's list included the dreamer's actual life history; the dreamer's memories of what has happened to him, especially during the past week; the "day residue" which includes immediate presleep experiences; and currently poorly understood factors such as atmospheric concentration, barometric pressure and paranormal stimuli such as telepathic messages.

The "Royal Road" to the Unconscious

In 1899 Sigmund Freud published his monumental work, *The Interpretation of Dreams*, in which he maintained that the dream is "the guardian of sleep" and "the royal road" to understanding man's unconscious.

How do the theories of Freud stand up today?

According to Dr. Krippner, experiments in sleep laboratories have confirmed many of Freud's speculations and cast doubt upon others.

Some psychiatrists, including Lester Gelb, argue that the concept of the unconscious should be totally abandoned in explaining human behavior. Gelb feels it would be more useful to recognize several states or types of consciousness--working, sleeping, dreaming, daydreaming, trance and so forth--each of which can be productively studied by behavioral scientists.

Possible confirmation of Freud's emphasis on sexual symbolism does occur in modern electroencephalographic dream research. According to Dr. Krippner: "Occasionally one comes across a dream so beautifully Freudian in its sexual symbolism and its goal of wish fulfillment that one is struck with the neat and precise manner in which it fits into Freud's theories."

Dr. Krippner further observed that while other dreams appear not to fit into Freud's system this should not be surprising. "We can scarcely expect any simple, unitary explanation of dreaming to be adequate. Human thought processes are too varied and complex for one approach to be completely sufficient."

Suppressed Traumas Surface in Dreams

Often when life experiences have become too emotionally painful to endure, they become suppressed and later surface in dreams.

Veronica Tonay, a doctoral candidate in psychology at the University of California, Berkeley, found that the dreams of women who had been sexually abused as children had become psychic battlegrounds wherein the women reexperience and refine the pain, humiliation, and trauma that they had suffered years before.

Continuing her research, which was reported in the April 1989 issue of *Psychology Today*, Ms. Tonay found amazing differences between the dreams of abused and nonabused women. The sexually abused women had many more dreams in which they were the victims of aggressive acts and violent attacks. The men in their dreams most often were represented as vicious animals. Many of the dreams portrayed sexual interaction. Other scenarios involved the neglect of children or depicted acts of harm directed at children.

Ms. Tonay goes on to report that patients who choose to undergo psychotherapy to help them deal with the memory of their abuse often have their emotional progress revealed to them in their dreams. After continued therapy many of the women come to "fight back" in their dreams, to shout at their aggressors or to resist them physically.

Dealing with Dreams Provoked by Memories of Abuse

If you are experiencing dreams of a type that you feel are related to early memories of abuse, keep careful track of them in your dream journal. Is there a symbol (bear, tiger, snake, etc.) that reoccurs more often than others?

In a relaxed state of mind, visualize either yourself or a dream character that you create to represent yourself, conquering an attacker in a manner most meaningful and most powerful for you.

Before falling asleep visualize the "conquering" scenario and tell yourself that if you have a dream in which you are being attacked that you will vanquish your foe in the manner that you have rehearsed. Actually see the new and desired ending to the dream step-by-step in your mind before you fall asleep. Program your dream computer to conquer your adversary.

Dream Dimensions

Dream researchers are not sure how the visual dimensions in dreams compare with the visual dimensions in everyday life. Dream reports indicate that most often the dream is on a "cinemascope screen" rather than on a small "television screen." People usually are seen full length and in about the same dimensions as they appear during waking hours.

Some dream researchers have noted the absence of movement during many dreams and suggest that dream imagery may be tableaux.

"One reason REMs (rapid eye movements) are associated with dreams may be that the eyes scan the visual scene just as they do during the waking state," Dr. Krippner commented.

> One subject had a high proportion of up-and-down eye movements as he dreamed of a person walking down a flight of stairs. Another had a high percentage of back-and-forth eye movements when he dreamed of a tennis match in which the ball was going back and forth across the net. On the other hand, eye movements also occur when the subject reports no movement in his dreams, suggesting that the relationship between rapid eye movements and dreams is highly complex.
>
> There is not a one-to-one relationship between waking time and dream time. However, extreme time distortion rarely occurs in dreams despite the fact that many psychologists used to believe that dreams lasted only a second or two.

The subjects at Maimonides' Dream Laboratory recalled the visual elements in their dreams most clearly, but auditory (sound) and tactile (touch) impressions also were common. Dr. Krippner says their dream reports resemble those collected by Herman,

Roffwarg and Tauber, who noted that 70 percent of their subjects' dreams contained specific sounds, 46 percent involved touch, seven percent taste and four percent smell. The ability to discern visual form (definitive shapes and boundaries) was present in 83 percent of the dreams; depth perception was noted in 78 percent and motion in 65 percent.

People Who "Never" Dream

While subjects in the dream laboratories report auditory and tactile impressions in addition to vivid visual dreams, some individuals stubbornly insist that they "never dream."

Since Krippner and other dream researchers have established that dreaming is as necessary to man was eating and drinking, it becomes apparent that the individual who claims he never dreams simply is not remembering his dreams. Dr. Krippner says

> If that person were to lie quietly in bed for a few moments each morning the final dream of the night would often be remembered. If he were to serve as a subject in a dream laboratory the experimenter would know precisely when the dream was occurring by observing the subject's REMs and could awaken him in the middle or at the end of the dream before he had a chance to forget it.

Archetypal Images

In Dr. Krippner's opinion, no dream symbols carry the same meaning for every person. Despite certain mass-produced "dream interpretation guides," the research in the dream laboratories indicates that only a very skilled therapist, working closely with an individual over a long period of time, can hope to interpret dream symbolism with any degree of correctness. Even then the therapist's interpretations would hold true for only that one subject.

Dr. Krippner points out, however, that certain dreams do occur with great frequency among peoples all over the world.

Dr. C. G. Jung spoke of "archetypal images" in man's

"collective unconscious." In this part of the mind, Jung believed, were images common to all people everywhere. People living in different times and different places have dreamed of "wise old men," "earth mothers," "mandalas" (circles within a square), and other "archetypes."

Dr. Carl Jung's theories are rejected by many psychologists and psychiatrists as being too mystical, but Dr. Krippner believes Jung's hypotheses really are not in conflict with what the dream researchers call "scientific common sense."

There must be something structural in the brain comparable to the structural form of other body parts. If so, this structure would develop along certain general lines even though an individual were isolated from other human beings. This may account for the appearance of 'mandalas' in many dreams; these shapes may well correspond to structures in the human eye and brain.

The Universality of the Dreams of Pregnant Women

Psychologist Patricia Maybruck, director of San Francisco's Neonatal and Obstetrical Research Laboratory, has discovered that thousands of the pregnant women whom she has researched have experienced the same types of dreams.

During the first trimester of pregnancy, women tend to dream of frogs, worms, and potted plants. Kittens and other cute, furry animals dominate the second trimester. Dreams of the final trimester feature lions, monkeys, and Barbie dolls.

Dr. Maybruck also learned that pregnant women often have the womb appear in dreams--most often symbolically as vessels, vehicles, or buildings. The more advanced the pregnancy, the longer and larger the dream image. Earlier in gestation the womb symbols may be closets, crates, or chicken coops. As the term progresses the symbols are elongated as trailers, leaning towers, and whole apartment buildings.

As Mary Roach reports in the May/June 1989 issue of *Hippocrates*, Dr. Maybruck also has discovered that pregnant women often spend a great deal of dream time on another very prevalent image: water. Whether in the form of oceans, lakes, rivers, or ponds, pregnant women dream a lot about water.

Carl Jung found water to be a universal symbol of generation and creation. If he was correct, then it certainly makes sense that dreams of water would be very much a part of the psyche of the woman who carries within her the creative energy of a new life. As might be expected, Dr. Maybruck found that the water in the pregnancy dreams became more and more turbulent as delivery time approached.

Dr. Robert Van De Castle, a clinical psychologist at the University of Virginia Medical School, also has conducted a great deal of research on the dreams of pregnant women.

> Physiologically, women are going through a pretty universal experience. They all have amniotic fluid so they are all going to be more tuned-in to watery content. They're all carrying a small, living organism within them....They're all going to get big bellies and start tipping backwards to balance the weight...so you're going to get tilted architecture.

Arthur Colman, professor of psychiatry at the University of California, San Francisco, and co-author of *Pregnancy: The Psychological Experience*, says, "People have extraordinary dreams when they are dying, and they have extraordinary dreams when they're pregnant. When you are going through an experience of a universal, mythic nature, your dreams are going to reflect that."

"Pregnancy, to many women, feels as though they're on a mild drug," Dr. Colman says. "There's enough reason just from the psychological state, but there's also some evidence that the increases in progesterone and steroids during pregnancy have a mood-altering effect."

Dr. Colman also points out that especially later in pregnancy women tend to awaken more often during the night and might, therefore, remember more of their dreams.

In Dr. Maybruck's study, 90 percent of the pregnant women had no fears or doubts or anxiety about their pregnancy--yet 40 percent of their dreams were declared to be nightmares.

"Pregnancy is a time of life crisis," she explains. "Pregnant women are experiencing more pressures and stresses than normal."

Because many women think they should acknowledge only joy and a kind of euphoria when they are pregnant, their sensations of discomfort or stress may cause them to feel a strange kind of guilt for not feeling better.

Some of the normal tensions of pregnancy may be dispelled by keeping a dream diary and by discussing the troublesome dreams with the woman's husband or family.

Dr. Maybruck states

> When we repress negative emotions, our bodies set up defenses to hold them in. We literally tense our muscles. When a women goes through six or nine months of holding in a lot of anxieties, it's going to be very difficult for her to relax--which is the key to a successful natural childbirth.

Nightmares

In 1968 R. J. Broughton complied considerable evidence that indicates that bed-wetting, sleepwalking and nightmares occur during periods of deep sleep rather than during periods of dreaming, as the layman often assumes. Bedwetting is common among unstable individuals, and the sleepwalker, in about 25 percent of the cases, is also a bed-wetter.

A nightmare differs considerably from a frightening dream. The terror of a nightmare is more intense and does not present an image or a dream sequence. The dreamer in the throes of a nightmare cries out while in deep sleep; he sweats and has dilated pupils, difficulty in breathing and appears as if paralyzed.

Dr. Krippner agrees that nightmares, bed-wetting and sleepwalking rarely coincide with dream periods.

Psychiatrist Ernest Hartmann of Tufts University believes that the nightmares of people who seem physically very healthy but who regularly suffer from "bad dreams" are reflecting their personalities rather than a traumatic past or a present struggle with health problems.

Dr. Hartmann found evidence of "thin boundaries" in people prone to recurrent nightmares. In his assessment they were men and women who tended to be more open and sensitive than the average. They were, he discovered, people with a tendency to become quickly and deeply involved in relationships with other individuals. At the same time, paradoxically, they also tended to be "loners," people who did not identify strongly with groups of any kind.

Dr. Hartmann developed a 138-item "Boundary Questionnaire" that he administered to over a thousand people, including a wide range of students, nightmare sufferers, and naval officers. The findings supported earlier studies that suggested that many of the men and women who endure nightmares are artistic or otherwise creative people. Naval officers, not surprisingly, most often turned up on the opposite end of the scale with rather "thick boundaries."

Dr. Hartmann speculates that "boundary thickness" may reflect a basic organizational pattern of the brain--one that is genetically determined or established early in life. The general openness of "thin-boundarized" people may predispose them to creativity, but it also binds them to a childlike vulnerability that leaves them at the mercy of the night creatures that go "bump" in the darkness.

Nightmares, then, just might be the price that some otherwise healthy and untroubled people pay for their sensitivity and creativity. The nightmare may work out the vulnerability, Hartmann states, especially if the sufferer learns to maneuver the frightening dream from a place of vulnerability to a place of control.

Keeping the Bogeyman Away!

After recording and identifying "patterns of vulnerability" in your nightmares, create in your mind your own dream script. It would be even better if you reinforced your screenplay by actually writing it down on paper.

Think of your worse recurring nightmare. Write the essentials of its "plot" down on paper, just as if you were penning the script of an academy-award winning horror film. The significant difference is that this horror film takes place in your own mind. This nightmare is not on "Elm Street"--it is inside your psyche.

Since you are the screenwriter, write your movie so that you are in charge. Identify the responses that make you feel helpless, and rework the scene so that you take over with unhesitating authority. You become a true "take charge" person, an "in-control" individual--yet still retaining an even greater creativity and a loving-kindness toward others.

Before falling asleep at night, go over your script in your mind. Imagine it. Feel it. Be it. Let it be completely and totally real in your sensitive Self!

Dreaming in Color

Until 1962 most dream researchers held that only a minority of individuals experience dreams in color. But such investigators as Kahn and his associates have reported that approximately 83 percent of all remembered dreams in their studies involved color. These findings have been confirmed by other researchers. In addition, some evidence indicates that intense emotion in dreams tends to be associated with color recall.

Dreams of the Blind

An area that has been little researched is dreams of the blind.

"The blind do dream," Dr. Krippner says, "but rapid eye movements do not accompany their dreams. The dream content does not involve visual imagery--rather it involves smell, taste, sound, touch and emotions."

In those experiments that have been carried out, the dream researcher had to distinguish between the dreams of those who were born blind and those who were blinded after a period in which they had experienced sight. Those who formerly had vision continue to dream in terms of visual imagery and REMs do not accompany their dreams. In addition, the dream time of the congenitally blind, according to Dr. Krippner, is rather brief.

Four Creative Aspects of Dreaming

Many artists, writers, inventors, musicians and other creative people have received inspiration in their dreams or have used their dreams as problem-solving catalysts.

Psychoanalyst Montague Ullman cites four creative aspects of dreaming:

1. the element of originality
2. the joining together of elements into new patterns
3. the concern with accuracy
4. the felt reaction of participating in an involuntary experience.

Dr. Ullman concedes that the final product of a dream's creativity may be either banal or ecstatic, but he insists that "it is an act of creation to have the dream in the first place."

Data currently being assembled indicates that dreams provide a fertile field for the examination of creative processes. The act of dreaming, that most personal and subjective experience, may well be a key to man's hidden powers.

A Dialogue with Dr. Stanley Krippner

What significance may there be in recurring dreams?

Dr. Krippner: Recurring dreams may be the result of several causes. An individual, because of past conditioning, may dream the same dream whenever he visits his childhood home, whenever he eats a certain food before retiring, or whenever the atmospheric conditions affect him in a certain way.

On the other hand, dreams may recur because they represent an unsolved personal problem or because they represent an unsatisfied wish. One man dreamed of being attacked by his mother until his psychotherapist helped him resolve the problem that was reflected in this dream. One woman frequently dreamed of a certain house until she owned a home of her own.

Dr. Krippner, can you tell us anything about those strange dreams wherein characters within the dream-drama constantly change into other characters? And then there are those dreams wherein characters appear in roles out of context. For example, your father might be seated beside you as a fellow pupil, or your old drill sergeant is playing jacks with your seven-year-old daughter. Is there any particular significance in such strange dreams?

Dr. Krippner: In many cases these unusual dream events may represent a chance phenomenon--a dream "collage" in which the individual's past memories combine in unusual ways, as do the stones in a kaleidoscope.

I know an adolescent who frequently has dreams in which his girlfriend changes into his mother. He has concluded that the two women have a number of characteristics in common and that the resemblance was one unconscious factor in the attraction he felt for the girl upon first meeting her. His dreams and his interpretation of their meaning have strengthened his relationship with the girl--as well as giving the boy a new type of appreciation of his mother.

Some people claim to have the ability to control their dreams, to direct the actions of those characters involved in their dream-drama. Others claim to be able to select their dream topics. Have you found any such subjects in your dream lab?

Dr. Krippner: We have found a very limited number of people who are capable of doing one of three things:

1. Some individuals can decide what they are going to dream before they go to bed. Their dream reports, if accurate, suggest that they often are successful in this   attempt.

2. Some individuals can remember a pleasant dream in the morning and decide to repeat the dream, or finish the dream, the following night. Once in a while, they are successful.

3. Some individuals can control a dream while it is going on. One man was being chased by a dragon. Suddenly he said to himself, "I am dreaming; it is silly to be afraid, I will make the dragon disappear." He waved his hands at the dragon and the animal disappeared.

Many experiments have been done with the hypnotic control of dreams. It is quite possible for a hypnotic practitioner to hypnotize an individual and have him imagine a dreamlike episode immediately. Some psychotherapists use this technique when their patients forget their dreams of the previous night. However, this dreamlike episode emerges from a different state of consciousness than does the nighttime dream and cannot be considered exactly the same.

Have you found any dream symbols that are common to our cultural group? Have you noted any dream symbols that might be considered universal?

Dr. Krippner: In my opinion there do not seem to be any symbols that carry the same meaning for every person. Dreaming of a king may represent a father for one dreamer, but to another dreamer the king may represent a desire for power. A third dreamer may have such a dream because he watched a television play about King Henry VIII just before retiring.

For some dreamers a long journey may represent a fear of death--but for others it may represent a desire to travel. Only a very skilled therapist, working closely with an individual over a long period of time, could interpret dream symbolism with some degree of correctness, and even then, his interpretations would hold true for only that one person.

On the other hand it is quite true that certain dreams occur with great frequency among people all over the world.

Plato was wrestling with this idea when he wrote that man is "born with certain ideas." A great artist, like Dante, Rembrandt or Shakespeare, taps the deep human levels of sorrow, joy, fear, and hope--producing classics that involve mental images and feelings that the individual artist possesses in common with other men in other times.

Furthermore, most societies have rich folk literature dealing with "wise old men" and "earth mothers." These images may influence the dreams--and in turn may be influenced by dream reports that have been related throughout the years.

People in various cultures have dreams that relate directly to their background as well as dreams that are "universal" in nature. Various primitive tribesmen will dream of serpent-gods, winged bulls, demonic spirits. These tribesmen also dream of less esoteric items that characterize the practical, everyday life of the dreamer. For example, a native living in the Amazon will not dream about snow; an Eskimo will not characteristically dream about the jungle.

During 1968 Robert Van de Castle collected dream reports from tribesmen in Panama and found their dreams to reflect the structure of the natives' everyday world as well as their mythological world. A great deal more research probably could be done in cultures around the world. Furthermore, this research needs to be done before television and other forms of mass media infiltrate primitive areas and broaden the entire range of the tribesmen's dream topics.

Is there some way in which each of us might learn to remember more of our dreams and what they may be telling us? Can you give us some suggestions on how we might examine our dreams for those things that may be speaking uniquely of our own inner lives?

Dr. Krippner: One primitive Malay tribe encourages each family member to discuss his dreams at breakfast. Other members of the family offer their interpretations. This type of constant examination of the inner life makes it easy for dreams to be remembered. It also may help account for the fact that this tribe does not engage in warfare; in addition, theft and mental illness are virtually unknown among tribal members.

By paying closer attention to one's dreams, an individual may gain a greater access to his inner life and, thereby, become a more sensitive, a more fully functioning individual. Specific suggestions might include the following:

1. *When you first awaken in the morning, lie quietly before jumping out of bed.* Let your mind dwell on the first thing that pops into it. Do not allow daytime interests to interrupt.

Your first waking thought may remind you of the contents of your last dream before awakening. You may need to try this technique several mornings in a row in order to get results.

2. *Keep a notebook of the dreams you do remember for a month.* Look for important ideas or themes running through the dreams.

You may discover that you have been working on a problem at night without being aware of it. You may even find instances in which your dreams suggested actions that you actually were able to carry out later.

3. *Look for items in your dreams that might be symbolic of something.* Avoid making hard and fast judgments. Get the opinion of your family and friends.

Remember, however, that it is more important that you enjoy the dream than correctly analyze it. It is more important that you learn to appreciate your inner life than that you become an amateur psychoanalyst.

4. *Look for puns in your dreams--a play on words, a play on numbers.* Word puns are common and often can be discovered.

5. *Before you go to sleep at night, review the work you have done on a problem or on a question that has you stumped.*

Concentrate several evenings in a row, if necessary. If you have given the problem enough presleep attention, you may find upon awakening in the morning that you remember a dream in which the possible solution appeared. This is one way of encouraging creative dreams.

6. *Keep dream diaries.* Record your dreams for six months or a year. Try to get other members of your family or your circle of friends to do the same. Determine as best you can which dreams reflected personal problems, which dreams involved national or international events, and which dreams were highly symbolic.

An exploration of your inner life may be as exciting and rewarding as your daily interaction with the external environment.

A Relaxation Technique to Help You Achieve Good Dream Time

The technique that follows is one of our favorites and it is almost guaranteed to place you in a deep sleep state so that you will have periods of good and productive dream time.

You may wish to have a family member or a friend read the technique in a soft, soothing voice while you fall asleep at bedtime. We also would suggest that gentle, restful music might be played at a low volume in the background.

Many people have stated that they like to read the technique in their own voice and record the process on tape so that they might play the cassette back at bedtime and allow their own voice to guide them through the relaxation procedure. They have told us that they feel that it is a very powerful experience to hear their own voice lulling them into a total state of relaxation and into a full receptivity to dreaming productively.

Either method can be effective, and your success will depend upon your willingness to permit such a process to manifest in your unconscious.

Visualize that at your feet there lies a soft, warm blanket the color of rose. It has been learned that the color of rose stimulates natural body warmth and helps to induce sleep. It also provides one with a sense of well-being and a great feeling of being loved.

Imagine that you mentally are moving the rose-colored blanket slowly up over your body.

Feel it moving over your feet, relaxing them. Feel it moving over your legs, relaxing them. Feel it moving over your stomach, removing all tensions...over your back, removing all stress.

With every breath that you take, you find that you are becoming more and more relaxed. With every breath you take, you find that you are becoming more and more dreamy, reflective, peaceful.

Any sound that you might hear--a barking dog, a slamming door, a honking car horn--will not disturb you. Any sound that you hear will only help you to relax, to sleep, to dream.

Now feel that you are mentally pulling the rose-colored blanket over your chest, your arms, relaxing them, relaxing them.

As the blanket moves over your neck, relaxing all the muscles of your neck, visualize the rose-colored cloth transforming itself into a hood that covers your head like a cowl. Now you are completely enveloped in the beautiful, peaceful rose-colored blanket, and you feel the color of rose permeating your psyche, enabling you to fall into a deep sleep, a sleep that will allow meaningful dreams--dreams that will teach you and enrich you.

The color green serves as a disinfectant and a cleanser. It also influences the proper receptivity of muscle and tissue to the healthful energy of deep sleep. Imagine that you are pulling a beautiful green blanket over your body.

Feel it moving over your feet, relaxing them, cleansing them, healing them.

Feel the lovely green blanket moving over your legs, healing them of all pains.

Feel it moving over your stomach, ridding it of all tensions.

Feel it moving over your chest, your arms...healing, relaxing, relaxing.

With every breath you take, feel yourself becoming more and more relaxed...more and more at peace, more and more at one with your mind and your body.

Feel the refreshing color of green moving over your back, relaxing all the stress along the spine. Feel the color of green cleansing, healing, relaxing your entire body.

As you make a hood of the green-colored blanket, pull it over your head, calming all of your nerves, your anxieties, your stresses. You are now completely enveloped in the healing color of green, and you feel it permeate your psyche, relaxing you, calming you, allowing you to have healthful dreams, positive dreams, teaching dreams.

The color of gold has long been recognized as a great strengthener of the nervous system. It also aids digestion, helps you to become calm, and allows you to have a deep and restful sleep.

Visualize now that you are pulling a soft, beautiful gold blanket slowly over your body.

Feel it moving over your feet, calming you. Feel it moving over your legs, relaxing them. Feel it moving over your stomach, soothing any nervous condition, healing any stomach upset. Feel the lovely, relaxing gold blanket moving over your chest, your arms, your back.

Nothing will disturb you, nothing will distress you. All stressful thoughts are leaving you. All concerns are being left behind as you become more and more relaxed...more and more relaxed...more and more prepared to have beautiful, golden dreams.

Feel the gold blanket fashioning itself into a protective hood that covers your head and completely bathes you in the color of gold. Feel the color of gold permeating your brain, your mind, your nervous system, permitting your body-mind network to create a healthier and happier you. Relax...relax...as you prepare to receive wonderful, golden teaching dreams from a Higher Intelligence.

Now visualize at your feet a blanket the color of blue. The color blue prompts psychic sensitivity and provides one with a sense of accomplishment and confidence. The color of blue will aid you greatly in receiving dream teachings of a positive and helpful nature.

Imagine that you are now willing the blue-colored blanket to move slowly up your body. Feel it moving over your feet, relaxing them. Feel it moving over your legs, your hips, relaxing them.

With every breath you take, you are becoming more and more relaxed...more and more ready to fall into a deep, deep sleep... more and more ready to dream wonderful, beautiful dreams. With every breath you take, you are more and more at peace...at one with the Universe.

Now you feel the blue blanket moving over your chest, your arms, your back...over your stomach, removing all tensions...over your back removing all stresses.

Everywhere the blue blanket touches you, you feel a wonderful, relaxing energy moving throughout every cell of your body. Everywhere the blue blanket touches you, you feel relaxed...relaxed...relaxed.

As the blue blanket becomes a beautiful blue cowl, imagine that the color of blue is about to permeate your psyche and give you the wisdom to accomplish all of life's important tasks in a positive way. Know that the color of blue will do its part in activating your dream machinery to produce dreams of a profound teaching nature. Feel the color of blue accelerating all of your psychic abilities.

Now bring the beautiful blue cowl over your head, and let it completely envelope you in its peaceful, relaxing, loving energy. Sleep...sleep...dream...dream...dream.

Chapter 2

To Know Your Dreams, Know Yourself

If dreams are the products of the subconscious mind, then those thoughts that we plant in the subconscious levels of our being become the realities of our lives, a potential source of dynamic power. While it may be true that dream material comes from various sources, including the superconscious, it still does not reach our conscious mind until it has been filtered through the subconscious reaches of the mind.

We all know the power of mind, and we see daily examples of it in the negative aspects of psychosomatic illness. We see the businessman who is ridden with ulcers, caused exclusively by worry about business matters. We see individuals driven to all sorts of physical illness that *began* in the mind.

If, indeed, the subconscious can work such negative actions, how many wonderful things can it accomplish when it is fed positive thoughts? What answers can we derive from the dream state once we learn how to program our minds to capture this information?

Dreams: The Royal Road to Integration

Fritz Perls, the founder of Gestalt therapy, believed that dreams were "the royal road to integration." In his view the various parts of a dream should be thoroughly examined and even role-played to gain self-awareness and to integrate fragmented aspects of the personality into wholeness.

According to Dr. Perls:

> All the different parts of the dreams are fragments of our personalities. Since our aim is to make every one of us a wholesome person, which means a unified person without conflicts, what we have to do is to put the different fragments of the dream together. We have to re-own these projected, fragmented parts of our personality and re-own the *hidden potential* that appears in the dream.

The Gestalt approach to learning about ourselves through dreams lies in a concerted attempt to integrate our dreams, rather than seeking to analyze them. This can be accomplished by:

1. consciously reliving the dreams
2. taking responsibility for being the people and the objects in the dream
3. becoming aware of the messages contained in the dream.

Dr. Perls found that in order to learn from our dreams, it is not essential to work out the entire dream structure. To work even with small bits of the dream is to learn more about the dreamer.

In order to "relive" a dream you must first refresh your memory of it by writing it down or by telling it to another person. Write it or tell it as a story that is happening now, in the present tense.

Dr. Perls uses the present tense in all of Gestalt dream work: "Dreams are the most spontaneous expression of the existence of the human being. Dreams are like a stage production, but the action and the direction are not under the same control as in waking life."

It might be helpful to visualize the whole analysis of dreams as a "script" from your own internal stage production. Include everything in the dream as you experienced it. Do not add any detail that was not actually there as you originally dreamed it.

For Step 1, then, you would use the present tense and say or write something like the following:

"I am sitting at my desk."
"I am driving down a lonely road at night."

For Step 2, you could ask yourself (as if in dialogue with yourself or with another person):

"What are you doing in my dream?"

Ask this question of every person and every object or event in the dream.

Then answer yourself in the first person. For example:

"I am a great big desk."
"I am a sleek new convertible."

Each part of the dream is likely to be disguised or to bear a hidden message about the dreamer. When the message comes through to you, you will feel that shock of recognition that Gestalt calls the "Ah-ha!"

Dr. Perls cites a case wherein a woman, seeing herself in her dream as a tyrannical, unbending employer, learned that she was, in fact, a very inflexible and unbending person, one who was unwilling to make changes in her life.

Another person, speaking from the viewpoint of the steam roller depicted in his dream, discovered that he had a tendency to "roll over" other people if he felt they got in his way.

The self-discovery in each of these examples enabled the "alienated personality fragment" of the dreamers to be "re-owned," and thereby integrated into the whole personality.

Dr. Perls issues a necessary caution:

If you work on dreams, it is better if you do so with someone else who can point out those things that you will avoid. Understanding the dream means realizing when you may be avoiding the obvious. The only danger is that the other person might come too quickly to the rescue and tell you what is going on in you, instead of giving you the chance of discovering yourself.

Dr. Perls concludes that every dream has a message to reveal to the dreamer. Like most dream researchers, he recommends that one keep a paper and pencil at bedside in order to record the important points of one's dreams as they are remembered. He suggests the following technique to assist in the recollection of dreams.

> * Write down the dream and make a list of *all* the details in it.
> * Remember every person, every object, every mood, and then work on these things to *become* each one of them.
> * Ham it up! Let yourself go and really become each aspect of the dream. Use your magic.
> * Don't hesitate to become that ugly frog! Turn yourself into whatever is in your dream--the live things, the dead things, the ugly things, the beautiful things.
> * Stop thinking! Act out your dream in as big a production as you possibly can.
> * Take each of the different items, characters, and aspects and have a dialogue between the two opposing parts of you. If you are able to ascertain the correct aspects of the opposites, you will find that they always start out fighting each other.

After you have worked through a dream or a dream fragment, ask yourself:

> "Was I avoiding something in the dream?"
> "Was I running away?"
> "Was I hiding?"
> "Was I unable to use my legs or my voice?"

Keep asking yourself questions until you feel that you have struck a responsive chord within yourself.

Has your dream fragment revealed a scenario with a set of circumstances that is similar to your real-life patterns or avoidances?

There is no need to become downcast after you have faced any negative aspects that you may have discovered in your dreams.

Remember, we all have suppressed negative fragments within us. Our goal should be that we may clearly see them and thereby learn more about ourselves so that we can get rid of the "garbage" that we don't want in our lives. It is through such a process that we may truly become whole, healthy, and happy!

We often learn more from our mistakes and our failures, so don't be afraid to explore deep within yourself. One of our favorite Chinese proverbs states: "The gem cannot be polished without friction nor man perfected without trials."

So go ahead. Don't be afraid to confront whatever may lie within the dream scenario. Just be prepared to be polished like the gem in that Chinese proverb. The more that you are polished, the more the real you can shine brightly!

Meditation Offers an Important Key to Dream Teachings

Although he had been well-known in parapsychological circles for years, Olof Jonsson gained international fame when he participated with astronaut Edgar Mitchell in the famous Apollo 14 ESP experiments from Moon to Earth in February 1971.

Olof Jonsson prefers a calm and peaceful place in which to condition his psyche for the kind of dreams that achieve his full potential. "I put myself in a light trance," he said, "then I can see what is coming into my life. I can see what is going to happen as if it is on a movie film. In my opinion, one can contact the Universal Mind when he is in this harmonious state."

Olof urges meditation as an important key to meaningful dreaming. He also recognizes good health as a contributing factor.

> I think you have to keep your mind and body in good shape. You should also train yourself to concentrate and remember things. You can control your dreams. If you want to dream about the future, you can put your mind there and dream about it. You can use your dreams to visualize those things you wish to occur.
>
> If you need an aid, lie down on your sofa or bed, close your eyes, and listen to some soft music, music you like. Allow yourself to go into a sleep. This will not be

a normal sleep, but a kind of trancelike sleep. It will allow you to place your mind into Universal Knowledge.

"Sleep on" Your Problems

Some of the world's most successful business executives never make a decision until they have a chance to let it pass through their minds during the hours of sleep, permitting solutions to come during dreams.

Once this practice of "sleeping on a problem" becomes habit, you will find that there is really nothing magical about it. It can become the route to personal achievement, success, and even wealth if your mind is so set. Whatever your goal may be, learning to use your slumber time will prove worth the effort of learning how to do so.

Dr. Norman Vincent Peale once suggested the following problem-solving plan: Learn to leave your problems at the bedroom door when retiring for the night. Put a small box on the door frame, and as you pass this on your way to bed, drop a note into it that briefly states your problems of the day--then forget them! The next morning, with practice, you will find that your problems have a way of solving themselves; the answers will be there, in your mind.

Remember, it is all a matter of training your mind to do certain things. The subconscious level of the mind is where we are working, not on the intellectual level. The subconscious has no sense of humor, understands symbols far better than words, and, in general, can be likened to an electronic computer. Material must be fed into it or it cannot produce effective answers. To the intellect it may sound silly, but to the subconscious it makes a lot of sense.

Know Thyself

The Number One rule in understanding your dreams is to understand yourself. It is only by knowing yourself as completely as possible that you will be able to identify and fully comprehend the dream symbols that are uniquely your own.

It is to that very special end that the checklists included in this book will constitute a kind of workbook that will permit you to understand those aspects of your personal universe that actually make the Real You tick. The questions are designed to enable you to perceive the true personality that you usually keep well-hidden behind all the protective mental/emotional barricades that you have erected.

While it is true that you might be able to rationalize the use of a few facades that you have constructed during desperate years of trial and error spent accumulating some painful Earth plane experiences, you must face the fact that your dreams deal with your *true* hopes, your *actual* aspirations, your *awful* fears. They have little to do with those careful responses that you launder before sharing with even those closest to you.

You know only too well that your dreams trot out all the nasty little secrets, all the embarrassing occurrences, all the blundering ineptitudes that you have sought to keep hidden in the darkened recesses of your psyche since the earliest glimmerings of your awareness of Self. At the same time, your dreams portray all your cherished goals of grandeur, all your favorite fantasies, and all of your hoarded illusions.

There is no hiding from your dreams, so if you wish to rank among the wise, you will learn to utilize that enormous creative dream power within your marvelous psyche. In order to gain total access to that most wonderful of inner resources, you must understand thyself as totally and as awesomely as is possible.

Understanding Personal Experiences
That May Contribute to Your Dream Scenarios

Take a comfortably deep breath, hold it for the count of three, then slowly exhale. Repeat this three times. Sit in quiet reverie for a few moments, then answer these questions as honestly as possible.

What are your earliest memories? _____

_____

When you believe that you have discovered your very earliest one, let your thoughts explore deeper. Can you discover any memories that may have been buried? _____

_____

Take a moment to experience these memories with your senses. What sounds, odors, touch sensations, tastes, and pictures are associated with them? _____

_____

_____

Holding the feelings from those memories in mind, reflect upon what sensory details have been most vivid in your experience during the past few weeks. _____

_____

Which of those details have you most enjoyed? _____

_____

Which have bored you or disgusted you? _____

_____

What was your favorite childhood activity before you entered elementary school? _____

_____

What was your favorite activity in high school or college? _____

_____

What is your favorite activity at the present time in your life?

_____

At those same stages--pre-elementary school, high school or college --what did you most dislike to do? _____

_____

What activity do you dislike most at the present? _____

_____

_____

What sports or physical activities have you enjoyed at some time in your life? _____

_____

Have you basically preferred organized or unorganized physical activities? _____

Do you remember any tense or stressful moments that were centered around a physical achievement in sports? _____

_____

_____

Do you remember any tense or stressful moments that arose around psychological conflicts of hate, rivalry, fair play, or the approval of others that were connected with your participation in sports?

_____

_____

What physical labor have you tried--and enjoyed or hated?

_____

_____

What troubles and fears have you had at different stages of your past? _____

_____

What has been your saddest experience in life? _____

_____

Whom did you admire most in your childhood before you entered elementary school? _____

Whom did you admire most in grade school? in high school or college? _____

_____

Whom do you admire most at the present time? _____

_____

Whom did you dislike most at the same stages--pre-elementary school, grade school, high school or college? _____

_____

Whom do you dislike most at the present time? _____

_____

Throughout the past, with whom did you get along better--your father or your mother? _____

With whom do you get along better today--your father or your mother? _____

How would you describe the kind of person with whom you would get along best? _____

Name the persons who have had a definite influence on you.

_____

_____

What do you consider to be the greatest personal problem with which you ever have had to deal? _____

_____

What do you foresee as the greatest problem in your future? _____

_____

What is the most difficult new situation that you have ever faced?

_____

Do you ever hide your true feelings about a situation? _____
If yes, why do you believe that you do this? _____

_____

Did you ever meet someone who forced you to feel inferior? ____

_____

Have you ever felt thoroughly ashamed of yourself? _____

_____

Have you ever experienced group disapproval? _____

Have you ever been disappointed because you did something well and failed to receive praise or approval? _____

Do you experience strong feelings of responsibility or duty? ____
_____

Do you consider yourself to be self-sufficient? _____

What is your true basis for really liking someone? _____
_____

What is your true basis for really disliking someone? _____
_____

Have you ever held an unpopular opinion or belief? What was the result of your taking such a stand? _____
_____

Have you ever courted favor from someone in authority over you? _____

Have you ever broken the code of behavior accepted by your family, friends, associates, or community? What were the results of your behavior? _____
_____

What is the heaviest physical labor that you have ever performed?
_____

What is the most exacting skill or task that you have accomplished?
_____

What was the most depressing or discouraging task that you have ever sought to complete? _____
_____

What has required the most strenuous effort of your will or perseverance?_____

Have you ever fantasized an ideal version of a situation-to-be, then bungled it terribly when it became real? _____

_____

Have you ever bungled a situation, then created an ideal version of the experience to tell others? _____

_____

Have you ever sought to find out something that was really none of your business? _____

Have you known a very painful moment of misunderstanding between yourself and a loved one or a friend? _____

_____

Have you known failure? _____

Have you experienced awful fear? _____

Have you been the victim of envy? _____

Do you truly seek to place your mind and your emotions in agreement with another? _____

During moments of introspection, have you discovered an inferiority complex or any other defense mechanisms within yourself?

_____

On what subjects are you aware that you will quite likely rationalize?_____

When it is just you sitting here all alone, what opinions or beliefs do you hold that are probably irrational prejudices? _____

_____

How do you usually react to small annoyances or irritations?

_____

In crisis situations, do you most often rise to meet the challenge --or do you become helpless and frightened? _____

Are you afraid of being alone? _____

Are there irrational ways in which you fear other people? _____

As you analyze your formal educational background, what influences in it do you now believe to have been of the most value to you? _____

What education influences do you consider to have been detrimental to you? _____

What informal education has been most important in your life?

What traits or interests do you have as a result of your informal education?_____

Examining Your Attitudes Toward Other People

What kind of person amuses you? _____

What kind of person is bound to antagonize you? _____

What sort of person really disgusts you? _____

What type of man or woman is certain to stir feelings of sympathy within you? _____

What sort of individual will be likely to rouse feelings of admiration within you? _____

Now try to find an actual person in your experience that fits each of the above categories and try to understand why that person has such an affect on you:

amusement _____

antagonism _____

disgust _____

sympathy _____

What kind of person do you dislike for no good reason that you can explain? _____

What actual individual in your experience have you taken an instant disliking toward for no sound reason? _____

With what kind of person do you get along best? _____

_____

Which people in your life have had the greatest influence upon you ? _____

_____

Which people have had an influence on you that at first you considered desirable, then assessed as truly undesirable? _____

_____

Do you feel that you are able to understand people whose religious, moral, political, or social ideas differ from yours? _____

_____

Which of your acquaintances seem to you to be the most popular? _____

What do you feel is the reason for that person's popularity?

_____

_____

Do you know anyone who at some time or another has shown one of these traits:

courage _____

stubbornness _____

greed _____

patience _____

loyalty _____

dishonesty _____

stinginess _____

determination _____

stupidity _____

superstition _____

provincialism _____

pride _____

Have you ever been in situations that brought out any of the above traits in yourself? _____

Learning How Your True Ideas About Things Affect Your Dream Teachings

What principles do you cherish so strongly that you would act on them spontaneously in the time of a crisis? _____

_____

Have you ever clashed strongly with your parents over such matters as religion or your occupation? _____

Have you ever had a serious confrontation with authority of one kind or another over your principles? _____

Do you feel that you have a sharply defined sense of integrity?

_____

Do you admire a strong sense of personal integrity in others, or do you prefer conformity in other people? _____

Have you experienced insecurity from external forces or circumstances, such as illness, death, drought, depression, war? _____

_____

What are your real beliefs about religion? _____

_____

How do you define God? _____

What are your real beliefs about survival after death? _____
_____

Have any of the above beliefs changed as you have grown older?
_____

Do you believe in cooperation or do you prefer unrestrained individualism?_____

Do you believe that happiness or love comes more readily from self-centeredness or from unselfishness? _____
_____

Set aside the conventional and accepted platitudes. What really makes you happy? _____
_____

Have you developed a basic philosophy about your place in the community? _____
        your place in the world? _____
        your place in the universe? _____

Have you developed a basic philosophy about
        the equality or inequality of husband and wife? _____
        responsibility for the children? _____
        the disciplining of children? _____

Do you think it is possible for a person to change his/her emotional nature or his basic behavior patterns? _____

Do you believe that you have some freedom in which to shape yourself and your own future, or do you really believe that it is only important that you *act* as though you had the freedom to shape your own destiny? _____

Do you recognize any forces that may impose limits upon you and your future? _____

What forces do you feel you may utilize to shape yourself and your future? _____

Discovering How Your Moods
Can Affect Your Dream Teachings

Have you ever been lonely at home, in a strange place, or in a foreign country? _____

What is the loneliest moment that you have ever known? _____
_____
_____

Have you ever left a place, hating to leave but knowing that you never would return? _____

Have you learned from your personal experience that "you can't go home again," that the home town doesn't stay the same? ___

Have you discovered from specific experience that friends change?
_____

Have you ever felt that you might have an incurable disease?
_____

Have you ever suffered a social stigma that you felt that you could never live down? _____

Have you ever known
    social insecurity? _____
    economic insecurity? _____
    the loss of a personal relationship? _____
    the loss of belief in religion? _____

Have you ever learned to your great dismay that you were inadequate when you so very much wished to be adequate in a particular situation? _____

Have you tried to appear self-reliant and sophisticated when you knew very well that you were neither? _____

Do you enjoy doing your best and giving your all for a cause or a charity? _____

Have you discovered any undesirable character traits in yourself?

_____

Have you discovered an undesirable character trait in another person whom you valued, so that you lost confidence in that person?_____

Have you ever discovered racial prejudice or some other prejudice in yourself of which you had been previously unaware? _____

_____

Have you ever been a victim of prejudice? _____

_____

Have you ever suffered a physical deformity or an accident or wound that made you conspicuous? _____

Have you ever felt frustrated and helpless because you couldn't make another person understand a moral or social principle that you had taken for granted? _____

Have you ever tried to defend a sensitive person? _____

_____

Have you ever watched a sensitive person suffer when you felt that you could do nothing to help? _____

Have you ever suffered because you were misunderstood? ____

_____

Have you ever harmed yourself by your own stubbornness? ___
_____

During your personal evolution and growth, have you changed
your attitude toward
      death? _____
      immortality?_____
      a religious belief? _____

Have you realized the smallness of individual concerns in contrast
to eternity, infinity, perfect truth and beauty? _____

Have you felt the transient quality of human life? _____
_____

Have you experienced satisfaction because you dared to be yourself
instead of following custom or convention? _____
_____

Have you ever felt
      hate? _____
      envy? _____
      triumph?_____
Do you feel any of those things now? _____
Why?_____

Have you ever tried to persuade someone to do something that
you knew was against that other person's principles? _____
_____

Have you ever enjoyed the rush of victory in a physical contest?
_____

Have you ever struggled with a fear of the dark? _____
_____

Have you ever been unhappy and unable to discover why? ____

Have you ever been completely happy and not been able to find out why? _____

Analyzing the Effects of Environment on Your Dreams

There is no questioning the impact of environment on the structure, form, and setting of our dreams. As we have already observed in this book, you must know yourself as fully as possible in order to gain the greatest value of the dream teachings that are available to you.

Answer the following questions when you know that you will not be disturbed for a rather lengthy period of time. Allow yourself to enter a reflective, introspective mood before you undertake the following analysis.

Have you ever entered a place when you were very tired and suddenly felt rested and rejuvenated? _____

What environmental setting most appeals to you at the present time?_____

Is there a place where you know that you would never want to live or to visit again? _____

Have you ever seen a house that you will long remember for its ugliness? _____

What place do you remember because it is associated with
former carefree days? _____
some other form of past happiness? _____
past sorrow? _____
a grandeur or a mystery that is now gone? _____

What is the ugliest landscape you know? _____

What is the most beautiful landscape you know? _____

Do you remember a place vividly where you
  struggled to gain a great victory? _____
  suffered a great defeat? _____

Do you remember a school that is closely connected with your
maturity and development--or perhaps a particular room within
that school? _____

Do you recall a church or synagogue that is closely connected
with your personal or family life? _____

Do you remember some historical spot or house clearly because
you learned something significant while you were there? _____
_____

What physical environments do you know well? _____
_____

What regions of the United States do you know well? _____
_____

What foreign places do you know well? _____
_____

What social class do you know best? _____

What other social class do you know well enough to contrast
or to compare with it? _____

What occupation or professional background do you know best?
_____

In the homes that you have known best, was the prevailing at-
mosphere due to the conscious or unconscious effort of one person's
effort or a group effort? _____

Of all the environments that you have known--physical, ethical,
psychological, social, educational, economic--which do you feel

have had the most desirable effects on you? _____

_____

_____

Which environments have had the most undesirable effects

      in your business or professional work? _____

      in your community? _____

      in your social group? _____

      among your closest friends? _____

Assessing the Effects of Your
Personal Philosophy of Life Upon Your Dreams

When crises arise in your life, what principles are you ready to act upon spontaneously? _____

_____

Do these principles concern your relationships to your

      mother and father? _____

      brothers and sisters? _____

      friends? _____

      community? _____

What basic attitude to religion or morals has been the prevailing one in your own life and in your family? _____

_____

What has been your basic attitude to

      work? _____

      money? _____

Have you disagreed with your parents or with other family members on any important questions? _____

_____

Have you differed with your friends on any important questions?

_____

_____

_____

Have you had strong disagreements with your business or professional associates on any important issues? _____

Are there any important questions on which you have not yet developed a personal philosophy? _____
If so, what are these questions? _____
_____
_____

Are there any important issues on which you have changed, even reversed, your basic principles? If so, under what circumstances did you change? _____
_____

Do you disagree on any important issues with the leaders--or with majority opinion--in your community? _____
_____

What things in the past have given you the greatest satisfaction?
_____
_____

What things do you believe will give you the greatest satisfaction in the future? _____
_____
_____

What beliefs, notions, or personal preferences do you have that are quite likely irrational prejudices? _____
_____

What or whom do you dislike for no good reason? _____
_____

Do you know well any person whose ideas--religious, moral, political, social--differ sharply from your own? _____
_____

Do you know well any person whose artistic or intellectual attitudes differ sharply from yours? _____

_____

How well do you think you understand the perspectives of this person?_____

_____

Do you know what he/she thinks of you and your opinions?

_____

Identify the specific fears that you have about the future. ____

_____

_____

Identify the specific hopes that you have for the future. _____

_____

_____

Keep a Meaningful Dream Diary

Keeping a dream diary is relatively simple. The hard part lies in disciplining one's self to make the daily entries--so start at the beginning by doing it right, the way that nearly all dream experts recommend.

* Immediately upon awakening, jot down your dreams on a note pad or dictate it into a tape recorder.
* Never put it off until later, for by the time you put on your slippers, take care of your toilet duties and sit down to breakfast, the dream will be long gone. Write it down *before* you get out of bed. (Of course, if you wake up during the night, capture any dreams that are fresh in your mind then, too.)
* Do not be concerned with penmanship or spelling--just get the facts on paper or tape. Later you can transcribe the material into your dream diary.
* Keep the diary simple. Write down the date, what the dream was about, and then leave a space for interpretation.

* Unless you can find an instant and logical meaning to your dream, put the diary away until you have more time to give it serious consideration. At least you have captured the essence of that dream.

Write That Dream Immediately!

Professor Nathaniel Kleitman, the distinguished University of Chicago physiologist and co-conductor of the Kleitman-Dement dream research findings, tells us that dreams are hard to remember because the higher centers of the brain are deactivated during sleep--or at least are operating at a much slower pace than during hours of consciousness.

The higher centers of the brain, those connected with thinking and memory, are in the cerebral cortex, that lining of the brain much akin to the rind of an orange. The cerebral cortex is the last part of the brain to develop in a child, the first to show signs of deterioration with old age, and the portion most affected by drinking. It is this portion of the brain that helps us make decisions, cull our memory of past events, and in general separates man from the slower animals by enabling him to reason.

Dr. Kleitman points out that the cerebral cortex operates at about half of its effectiveness when we are engaged in monotonous routine functions such as washing dishes, driving a car, or any other laborious job that is performed more by rote than by cunning.

The cerebral cortex is that portion of the brain that selects, abstracts, sorts, and memorizes when it is fully activated; but when the rest of the body sleeps, it, too, takes a nap, and that makes the memory of dreams a bit difficult at best.

The memory of dreaming, then, must in some way awaken the cerebral cortex, on cue, so that we can better remember what we dream. The habit of writing it down immediately upon awakening will, to a degree, help set the cortex on the alert so it can go into action on a moment's notice.

Keep It Simple

Roger Chappel, a Spiritual Frontier Fellowship member from Rock

Island, Illinois, has spent a great deal of time applying himself to the challenge of dream interpretation. Roger was willing to share the following with dream researcher David Graham:

> The keynote is always to *keep it simple*. Too often people seek the sophisticated, the unusual, the glamorous, the sensational, and they like to describe their dreams.
>
> I share the view that there are basically only three types of dreams:
>
>> Those that are duly nonsensical.
>> Those that are truly prophetic.
>> Those that directly relate to the thought patterns from the day before or recent past, offering solutions or insight to problems, anxieties or whatever.
>
> It is my opinion that the bulk of the dreams fall into this third category.
>
> A good place to start the interpretation process would be a close examination of the daily activities of the immediate and recent past. Then by employing (in a state of relaxation) common sense with perhaps some intuition added, a good, accurate analysis can be obtained.
>
> One of the best ways I have found to remember my dreams is to tell myself before going to sleep that I am going to remember my dreams and immediately record the dream upon awakening.
>
> In the beginning you may only be able to remember one word or scene. Keep a pencil and paper beside your bed and *write it down*! Within a week or two you will be surprised that you will be able to remember entire dreams that will cover several pages. Once your other levels of consciousness realize that you are serious in wanting to remember your dreams, it will not take long for it to happen. You, of course, record the dream as it was dreamed and interpret it later.

Each person must develop his or her own dream vocabulary.

This simply means a particular symbol for you will not read out the same for everyone. Standardized dream dictionaries may be helpful at times, but you must develop your own symbolic vocabulary that will be yours alone.

With patience and simplicity, you can have a fairly complete vocabulary that will allow accurate dream analysis and improved daily living within six months.

Each time you attempt to interpret a dream, record the matched-up words and symbols that you feel are correct. The entire dream does not have to have been interpreted accurately in the beginning so long as you are able to get some of it correct. With this process you gradually will develop a collection of matched-up words and symbols that can, of course, be applied to future dreams.

Obviously, the more you practice using this procedure, the more complete and accurate your efforts will become.

Chapter 3

Exploring the Parameters of Your Dreamscape

Oscar Luther had had the dream quite early in the evening of March 3, 1940, and it had so disturbed him that he was unable to sleep again that night.

He had seen three boys drifting down the Zumbro River in the water tank that they had commandeered for a boat, just as he had read about it in the newspaper. The tank had tipped over, sending the Rochester, Minnesota, teenagers into the cold water.

Two of the boys had made it to shore, but 14-year-old Gordon Reiss had drowned; his body had been carried two miles downstream where it now lay partially buried in a sand pit.

But how could Oscar Luther know where the body lay? The local newspaper headlined the fact that the boy's body remained *undiscovered* after a two-day search.

Luther sat up in bed for the rest of the night and pondered his mysterious dream.

A partial invalid, he had never been walking along the banks of the Zumbro River and certainly had never seen the area in which the boy had drowned. But, he shook his head, it all seemed so real. As if the corpse itself had given him the message.

Early the next morning, he called Fire Chief C. E. Ginther, the man who had been directing 60 volunteers in the search that had begun on the Saturday afternoon the Reiss boy had drowned.

"Chief," Luther began. "this may sound weird, but I know where you can find the body of Gordon Reiss."

"Who is this?" Ginther snapped, suspecting that a prankster

with a weird sense of humor might be at the other end of the line.

"This is Oscar Luther. I don't know how I know this, but I know it. I can even draw you a map of the area."

"But aren't you the...."

"That's right," Luther interrupted. "I'm the fellow in the wheel-chair. Last night when I went to bed, I knew no more about the drowning than what I had read in the newspaper. Now, this morning, I know everything there is to know about the tragedy--including where the body can be found."

Despite his strange story, Luther's obvious sincerity and intelligence convinced Ginther to send a man over for the map.

Late that afternoon, using the crudely drawn map as a guide, George Wood discovered the body, half-buried in the sand at the exact spot Luther had indicated.

"It was incredible," Wood said. "Luther had never seen the site in his life, yet his map of the area was completely detailed and correct in every way."

Reaching Beyond the Limits of Self

The more that you begin to understand that your inner dreamscape has marvelous terrain filled with undiscovered treasures, the more aware you will become that you are part of something so much bigger than yourself, so much larger than all of humankind amassed.

As you progress in your exploration of your dreamscape, you will find yourself reaching beyond the material aspects of yourself and tuning in to an intelligence that appears to fill all of space.

As you become stronger in your dream power, you will increasingly discover that communication can take place with a total disregard for distance. Prayers will be answered, and problems will begin to diminish.

Dream Power Exercises

The added wonder of your receiving dream teachings will be the discovery that your body is becoming less subject to the stresses that you have previously imposed upon it.

Preparatory to exploring your dreamscape, lie in your bed in an attitude of quiet meditation and attune yourself to the Blessed Intelligence that governs the Universe. Whenever you find yourself spending a few moments in quiet attunement, you are helping to undo the restricting attitudes of separateness between yourself and the Cosmos and you are permitting Divine Energy to flow more easily through you.

A good exercise to repeat on a daily basis to demonstrate physically and audibly your ability to join the Seen and the Unseen is to stand with your arms stretched forward, your palms upward, and intone the universal sound "Ommmmmm" in a long, drawn-out flow.

Repeat the Ommmmmm until you actually feel tingling in the palms of your hands--until the skin actually picks up auditory vibrations.

Then begin to project another type of energy toward your palms. Try to project a life force to your palms.

Visualize the life force passing through your fingers, moving out to the palms of your hands. Focus on this until you begin to feel a tingling sensation--almost as if electrical vibrations are moving through you.

Next, begin to feel an actual, palpable force moving out of your palms. Visualize a golden ball of energy hovering just beyond your palms. Know that this is an energy of Love, an energy of Love that you are able to project to others.

Visualize that golden ball moving through the walls, through the ceiling, through space, and see it enveloping someone whom you are imaging in your mind.

Visualize your golden globe of Love surrounding that individual. See the love flowing from your internal energy source, moving out from your palms, manifesting in the golden globe, then touching someone with connective energy.

This is an excellent technique by which you may practice the projection of your thoughts. This is a very effective exercise to practice before falling asleep so that you might more readily attain the goal of telepathic dreams--touching someone's consciousness with yours while in the sleep state.

Techniques of a Master Teacher

Roy Eugene Davis, a well-known teacher of spiritual realities, has these words of advice to share regarding the exploration of one's personal dreamscape.

Meditation and inspirational reading just before sleep aids this process. One can have "contact" with enlightened persons in dreams--either a real contact or a fabricated one, with the message still useful. Also, one can communicate with another person via dreams (sometimes this is "wish fulfillment," to be sure).

At other times, I feel we either telepathically communicate, and the dream results to firm up the communication; or we actually function on the astral plane and communicate on a subtle level. We can, of course, see into the future (and the past) in this manner.

Another method, taught by mystics, is to *watch* ourselves move from the conscious level to the sleep state and *be aware*. In time, we can remain aware even while sleeping and experience the "fourth state" which lies beyond (or to one side) of sleep, dreams, and waking states.

Yogic method is to "expect" to be conscious during dreams. The time will come when we actually are aware while dreaming, and know, "I am dreaming." We can then participate and observe--or we can, through mild desire, alter the dream sequence. We can also "turn" the dream into color, or make it black and white. After sleep we can recall the conscious-witness attitude we had while dreaming and compare it to our "waking dream" experience, that is, our ordinary conscious life.

Yoga masters teach that everything (all cosmic manifestation) this side of the Absolute non-dual aspect of Consciousness is taking place in universal mind and is, therefore, God's dream.

The Spiritual Dimensions of Dreams

For many years we were engaged in a fascinating correspondence with Dr. Ingrid Sherman, a noted teacher, counselor, and lecturer who conducted the Peace of Mind Studio in Yonkers, New York. As well as having gained a considerable reputation as a spiritual psychologist, Dr. Sherman was widely recognized as a poet who had developed a form of poetry therapy that was utilized with great success in institutions and hospitals throughout the world. But it was as a metaphysician who had spent an enormous amount of time pursuing the subtleties of dream studies that Dr. Sherman supplied the following notes from her journals.

In addition to what one may term "regular dreams," there exist those which I call "Dreams of Different Dimensions."

1. *Revelations from Former Incarnations*: These dreams bring us back in Time and Location. They are very useful, as they shed light on some former lifetime occurrences or problems that have a certain effect on our present situation. By recognizing this fact, one can work toward more desirable developments and positive goals.

2. *Spiritual Dreams*: In these dreams the dreamer feels elated, high-spirited, divinely inspired, God-conscious. He meets saints and sages from the higher planes, according to the dreamer's own conscious level. Many a spiritual person has seen the face of the Blessed Mother, Jesus Christ, a famous guru or master, a prophet of the olden days, a known religious leader, and other such great spiritual people.

In these dreams, the dreamers are sometimes given Bible quotations or referrals to certain Bible pages. I have received psalm numbers to look up, and when I do, the indicated psalm always carries a definite meaning to help me or others. Spiritual dreams, *per se*, have the strength to open to us the doorways to the Oneness with God and the Universe.

3. *Psychic Dreams*: In these dreams, spiritual, or so-called psychic, healings can take place, actually occurring in the dream and being watched by the dreamer. Such healings come about through the higher planes of existence without medical instruments.

4. *Clairvoyant-Telepathic-Prophetic Dreams*: In these dreams one experiences a certain condition taking place that will actually happen in reality at the time of the dream or at a later date. This can involve a house burning down, a family member in danger, a landslide, a flood, an earthquake, etc. In such dreams, also, the numbers of horses, lottery and raffle ticket numbers which are winners will be announced, along with other correct forecasts and prophecies.

5. *Precognition and Retrocognition*: The above takes place in dreams during sleep. It is received through non-sensory means either before (*pre*) or after (*retro*) a certain event takes place.

6. *Astral Projection or Astral Travel*: This is the travel of the astral body leaving the physical form and projecting elsewhere while retaining Earth-consciousness. Such experience occurs to people during their sleep state.

Dream Explanations and Interpretations

According to the Jewish tradition, to clear a bad dream was deemed important enough to follow it with a "Fast Day," even on the Holy Sabbath.

Dreaming that one is naked depends upon the place of dream. In old Babylon it was a sign of purity, meaning "free from sin."

A dream of snakes or pigs may suggest that we are surrounded by enemies.

Some troublesome scenes may repeat again and again. Heed them; they will teach you something worth while.

Sometimes malfunction in the body system is pointed out in a dream. Check it through. You may be spared much worry and extra expense for a doctor!

In *healing dreams* an actual healing takes place during sleep, or a certain cure may be recommended. Dreams during periods of high fever sometimes promote quick and spontaneous healings. Personally, I dream of remedies that cure other peoples' ailments.

I have coined the phrase "As a man dreameth, so he is!" because I feel that a dream is oftentimes more truthful than the dreamer is to himself in real life.

Through dream evaluation we can come to self-realization, self-understanding, and self-knowledge, as well as better understanding of others and the world around us.

Dreams serve as guideposts through which many a man has been led to his proper goal and thus created a healthier, a better, and a happier life for himself and for others!

Dr. Sherman's Helpful Instructions

1. Fully relax mind and body.
2. Keep the mind clear of impure thoughts.
3. Be in a receptive mood for dreams to appear.
4. Have a pad and pencil by your bedside.
5. Ask the Lord before you retire for an answer to your problem through a dream.
6. Say a prayer and ask to be helped to remember in detail all about the dream.
7. Thank the Lord in advance for helping you via a dream.
8. Slowly arise in the morning, sit for a while on the edge of your bed and reflect, remembering your dream from the night before.
9. Write it down and either interpret it yourself or have it done by someone competent.

Had Any Spaghetti Dreams Lately?

John Catchings, the brilliant psychic crimebuster from Texas, identified the boundaries of his dreamscape along the following lines of demarcation:

> I believe that most dreams can be broken down into three types: Reincarnation dreams, Spaghetti dreams, and Psychic dreams.
>
> *Reincarnation dreams* are the dreams that we all have at times which can be traced to recall from a past life experience. Usually these dreams come to us as pictures of a past time, as if they were from a history book. We may see ourselves, or images that seem to be ourselves, dressed in costumes of the past during a reincarnation dream.
>
> *Spaghetti dreams* are the dreams which we may have if we eat or drink too much. They are always meaningless and are similar to the ravings of someone on a drug trip.
>
> *Psychic dreams* are the dreams which help us understand the future and understand ourselves. There are three types of Psychic dreams. They are Subjective dreams, Physical dreams, and Spiritual dreams.
>
> *Subjective dreams* may have an element of prophecy or warning. These dreams may come in symbols, or with a hidden meaning. If you were to dream of an automobile accident, this could be a warning to be careful of your health in the days to come. This would be a subjective dream.
>
> *Physical dreams* are usually a reflection of something that has been worrying you, and should not be confused with subjective dreams.
>
> These dreams are a lot like spaghetti dreams and are very seldom accurate. They are usually brought on by worry or ill health. If you were to dream the night before an important exam that you failed the exam, do not consider this a prophecy, but only the manifestation of your own worry.
>
> *Spiritual dreams* are dreams of the highest psychic level and usually involve some type of communication. For example, if you were to receive a message from a close friend or member of your family during a dream, then this would be a spiritual dream.

Another example would be a dream during which a teacher would come to you with helpful information. Often I have been given information during a spiritual dream. I have been given instructions about my own future. In these dreams an older man comes to me with the information, or else it is a relative to whom it was close who is now in the spirit world.

Night Classes in the Halls of Learning

Bev DiSorbo Barney, an authority on dream study from Phoenix, Arizona, maintains that to explore the parameters of one's dreamscape is to bring true power into one's life. She points out that the Scriptures emphasize that God chooses to reveal himself chiefly in dreams. It seems apparent to her and to other researchers that the reason for this lies in the fact that the human spirit is more receptive to Divine influences and messages in the dream state.

The following (as she prepared them for one of our earlier publications) are Bev's thoughts on how best to receive teachings in the "Night Classes in the Halls of Learning":

Studying one's dreams is **power**. Through the mastery of dream codes we are enabled to *see inwardly*, thus recognizing and coming closer to the God mind (Higher Self, superconscious, God-within--or whatever you may want to term it), of which we are all a part. *Therein lies all power*. There is no braver venture than the study of one's self. It takes greater courage to look inside yourself than anything you may ever attempt.

When first exploring dream time it is *critical* that students obtain an honest understanding of their own dream symbology.

Let's say four people dream of a cat. The first person loves them. The second person experiments on cats in a laboratory, the next fears them, and the fourth is allergic to them. It only stands to reason that a cat would have a completely *different* meaning to each. This is why it is important that one seeks to interpret dreams from an *inward* consciousness rather than an outer awareness.

Remember, no one can interpret your dreams successfully but *you.*

In the beginning of serious dream study, many of my students find it most effective consciously to program dreams in which they attend "Night Classes" in the "Halls of Learning," visit the Akashic Records, or enter the universal consciousness of the collective consciousness. Such a process of tapping into the universal data bank may be used in re-enforcing a specific talent or ability as well.

Learning at night is hardly a new concept, but programming and controlling that learning for the conscious level can greatly enrich and give **power** to one's life in any area.

When working at night with dreams, one can actually control the psychic energy of disease (dis-ease) and change the current to a healthy one. Researchers all over the world are finding success with this process on conscious levels, so it's only logical to use it on a higher one.

I maintain an active conscious life and find it most useful to use my dream time for learning, working out challenges, and healing.

A beginning dream program might go like this (It's most beneficial to make up your own programming to fit your individual needs):

"Tonight as I sleep, I desire to attend night class on the study of my own dream symbology. I want to know what I am dreaming while I sleep. I want to understand the dreams that are significant to me on a conscious level."

It is not important that you remember these classes, although many of my students attend them together over the week and talk about them in class. The information you seek **will** be available to you when you need it. With each positive suggestion you give your unconscious mind, live in the law of *expectancy.* Believe and really know your programming will work.

I suggest *Dreams: Your Magic Mirror* by Elsie Sechrist; *Creative Dreaming* by Patricia Garfield, Ph.D. and *Dreams*

Sharing by Robin Shohet, using Ann Rae Colters' *Watch Your Dreams* as a guide to interpretation. These authors will lead you to others.

I also like my advanced students to be familiar with *all* the Seth books by Jane Roberts, *Living Your Dreams* by Gayle Delaney, *Dreams: God's Forgotten Language* by John A. Sanfor, *How to Interpret Your Dreams* by Mark A. Thurston, Ph.D., and *Edgar Cayce on Dreams* by Harmon H. Bro, Ph.D., under the editorship of Hugh Lynn Cayce.

The most meaningful tape I have ever discovered on using dream time to enhance your life happens to be by Brad Steiger. I highly recommend *Using Your Dreams to Shape a More Positive Life*, exercises in dream creativity by Brad. His keen insight to the subject matter, his consummate teaching manner and mastery of mind take you on an incredible journey within. Step by step the author creates a state of deep relaxation, but also of profound awareness. He offers to lead you through the wonderful world of the *inbetween universe* to the three greatest vibrations of the universe--*love, wisdom, and knowledge.*

In class, students consider working on the subject of *forgiveness*. Such an effort is a prerequisite for my Dream Study I class, as it is impossible for us to grow in the exploration of "inner life" unless we learn this gentle art. *forgiveness* is the most healing thing you can do for yourself, and it can be accomplished in dream life.

Just before falling to sleep, take a few moments and stretch your body. Do this lying down.

Reach upward with your hands...stretch outward lazily...roll about until you feel your spine relaxing. Breathe in deeply...*hold*...slowly release your breath, following it as it comes out.

Again, breathe in, feeling the energy as you do so. Feel it going deeper and deeper. Follow it as it goes up into your head, down through your arms and body and into your legs.

Feel your body tingle as the energy flows deeper with each breath. Now visualize the energy flowing with each exhalation out of every pore in your body.

As you practice this, visualize your breath pushing out all tension, anxiety, and any negative emotion you may be experiencing at this moment. Continue until you feel completely cleansed.

Choosing to forgive unlocks the doorway to all good. "Every time we forgive, we forgive not only for ourselves but for All."

Now close your eyes and begin to focus your attention on those in your life needing forgiveness. As they crop into your mind, silently bless them and concentrate on the lesson they brought to you, rather than the hurt.

Do not rush this exercise. Continue to look at the situation until you get past the anger and resentment to the *lesson*. Then simply release them *after* you have forgiven them, genuinely. Do not go on until you can completely and lovingly release them first.

This process can take months or longer in some cases. Things you've forgotten from childhood will begin to pop up as you get comfortable with the process. You are beginning to take control and shape your world with new healthy attitudes, leading to greater fulfillment, more abundant living, inner peace, and most of all, *healthier* living by choosing to forgive.

Now you are ready for your dream program:

"I recognize that as I forgive, I am forgiven. Tonight in the dream state I take the opportunity to meet with and forgive and release this situation, realizing the gift (lesson) it has brought to me. I express love toward myself, then to _____, and in this way I contribute to my own progress. I now begin anew, and become wiser, happier and healthier.

(Again, I suggest you be creative and use your own wording, applying it to you and your life).

You may want to write your program down on a card and repeat it over and over as you lay in bed. Some record their program several times. A message to your Higher Self in your own voice is *most* effective.

Programs can be made up to bring dreamers lucid,

reincarnational, health, sex, and mass dreams. You can develop dream guides, seek gifts, and create a more satisfying life experience along the way.

These exercises will help you to obtain the *power* offered in dream life. This study takes dedication and objective observation on your part. *Above all else you must be honest with yourself.* The whole purpose of harnessing dream life is *growth*.

To cease to grow is to relinquish our own "Self-power."

Chapter 4

Preparing for Dream Teachings

Dreams, visions, and inspirations are all best achieved by entering sleep time or meditation with the proper goals held foremost. Dream teachings, visions of guidance, and creative inspirations are all best attained by sincere and respectful journeys into that area of consciousness that American Indian medicine people refer to as "the Silence."

In the Silence, according to this cosmology, the most holy of energies are concentrated. When you enter the Great Silence, you will feel and know that it is composed of the vibrations of Cosmic Light.

To receive creative impulses from the realms of the Higher Self, as channeled through your dreams or your meditations, is to become the focal point for the most powerful energy that you can ever receive. The essence of the Silence is Light and Love, and pulsating deep within this luminous energy is the essence of the Source-of-All-That-Is: God.

Feel the Sacred Energy of the Silence

Prior to your seeking a dream teaching, sit or lie quietly and concentrate on feeling the energy of The Silence touch you. *Feel* the essence of it focused in your spiritual center (visualized for mental assistance as your Crown Chakra, the top of your head) and in your physical center (visualized for mental assistance as your Heart Chakra).

Take three comfortably deep breaths and *know* that the Sacred Energy of the Silence has permeated the spiritual and physical focal points of your own essence. Be still--within and without --knowing that the Power of the Silence has entered all levels of your consciousness and all levels of your being.

Take three comfortably deep breaths, holding each for the count of three. Feel at one with the essence of the Silence that has blended with you.

Visualize a bright, golden flame in your Heart Chakra. In your mind, imagine a ray of golden light traveling from your Heart Chakra to your personal concept of the Source-of-All-That-Is, to the very Heart of the Universe. See points of violet light touching every cell of your physical body as your light begins to connect with your own Higher Self. Begin to sense strongly a closeness, an at-one-ment with the Source.

Concentrate for a moment on making your body as still as possible. Direct your attention to the Source and focus on the flame within your Heart Chakra. See clearly the ray of light that you are transmitting to the Source.

Feel your consciousness melding with Higher Consciousness and eliminate awareness of your physical body as your connection to Earth and nothing more.

Visualize yourself holding open hands to the Source, as if you were about to receive some object of material substance. Now begin to request a dream teaching from the Highest Source-of-All-That-Is.

Mentally affirm the following (or create your own variation in keeping with the essence of the following supplication): "Source-of-All-That-Is, give to me a dream teaching that will inspire me with strength, energy, and great creative power. Grant that the dream teaching that I receive will show me those things that I need to know for my good and for my gaining."

Visualize the Source as the eternally powerful energy source that ignites the golden flame that burns within your own Heart Chakra. The more clearly, the more profoundly, that you can visualize this connection, the greater the results of your dream teaching.

The Pebble in the Pool

Here is an excellent technique for helping you to expand your consciousness just before falling asleep and entering the dream state.

Visualize a great pool of water before you. The pool is somewhere in the great out-of-doors, perhaps in a forest at the foot of majestic mountains.

See yourself as if you were a pebble tossed by some great cosmic hand into the pool. Allow your consciousness to become the ripples that spread across the surface of the pool. See the ripples of consciousness moving farther and farther across the surface of this great pool.

See your consciousness rippling from the center of the pool to the farthest horizon, moving, moving onward until your ripples have formed a great circle. You are in the center, spreading forth with the great ripples of expanding consciousness. You are in the center, but like a great circular pool, you have touched all points of the horizon--east, west, north, south.

You feel the circle of your awareness growing larger and larger until it touches the furthermost points of the horizon. You are aware of yourself as only a focal point in the midst of the great pool of Time, the great pool of Creative Energy.

Open your heart to the blessings that will return in the ripples that come back from each horizon. Let your essence return to the pool of Creative Energy. Receive ripple after ripple of greater consciousness returning to the center of your awareness.

Reaching Beyond the Physical Body

The Cosmos works according to Divine Principles, whether we know, understand, and accept them or not. The more that you reach beyond your body and explore the new boundaries available in dreams, visions, and inspirations, the more that you can tap those same principles. Simultaneously, your body will become less subject to the stresses that you impose on it.

With your new increased consciousness, you will come more

and more to stand in the Light, and you will wonder why others around you--who are less aware--are complaining about the darkness.

Living in the Light

Spiritual teachers have long been able to harness the energy of Light in a metaphysical way. Jesus, Mohammed, Saint Paul, and numerous other saints, masters, and spiritual heroes have experienced the Divine Light in its tremendous intensity. Here is a simple exercise to help bring about illumination and the manifestation of the Divine Light of Creativity in your dreams and in your day-to-day life.

Relax very deeply in the privacy of your room. Conduct a two-minute process of visualization in which you envision a brilliant light surrounding your head, surrounding your body.

Visualize that light moving around you. You know that the light has come from the very heart of the Universe. You know that it is the light of goodness. It is the light of unconditional love.

Visualize that light moving into you. Visualize that light actually becoming a part of you. Visualize yourself becoming at one with the light.

Now as you lie down to sleep, to dream, visualize yourself as a Light Being. Permit the light from the very heart of the Universe to guide your Essential Self to receive dreams of great illumination and powerful creativity.

Know that you have the ability to receive powerful teaching dreams of illumination and light.

Receiving Dream Teachings

The best way to consider the creative visualizations in this book is as "dress rehearsals" for your dreams. It is possible to program your dreams in the sense that you can rehearse the appearance of various symbols to manifest in your dreams and you can prepare yourself to recognize them as signalling the advent of dream teachings.

One of the most basic mechanisms for the receiving of dream teachings is your developing a mental construct of a guide or a wise teacher who will provide you with important information that can assist you in your day-to-day trials and tribulations. You may visualize this wise teacher translating guidance from your own Higher Self, or you may wish to believe that you are truly making productive contact with an angel, guide, or spiritual teacher in your dreams. Who is to say that you are not?

It is possible for you to read the relaxation technique, pausing now and then to permit its effectiveness to permeate your essence. It is possible for you to read the visualization for spiritual contact, pausing now and then to ponder the significance of your inner journey and to receive elevation to that higher spiritual realm.

You may wish to read the technique to another, permitting that individual to accomplish spiritual contact. Then, later on, that same friend may assist you in reaching a state of deep relaxation and assist you to establish your own linkup.

It also is possible to record your voice, reading these techniques onto a cassette tape, so that you might play the tape back and allow your own voice to guide you through the relaxation process and through the heavenly realm.

Any of these methods can be effective. Your success will depend upon your willingness to permit such an experience to manifest in your consciousness.

Imagine that you are lying on a blanket on a beautiful stretch of beach. You are lying in the sun or in the shade, whichever you prefer.

You are listening to the sounds of Mother Ocean, the rhythmic sound of the waves as they lap against the shore. You are listening to the same restful lullaby that Mother Ocean has been singing to men and women for thousands and thousands of years.

As you relax you know that nothing will disturb you, nothing will distress you, nothing will molest you or bother you in any way. Even now, you are becoming aware of the Golden Light of Love, Wisdom, and Knowledge that is moving over you, protecting you.

You know you have nothing to fear. Nothing can harm you.

As you listen to the sound of the ocean waves, you feel all tension leaving your body. The sound of the waves helps you to become more and more relaxed.

You must permit your body to relax so that you may rise to higher states of consciousness. Your body must relax so that the Real You may rise higher and higher to greater states of awareness.

You are feeling a beautiful energy of tranquility, peace, and love entering your feet; and you feel every muscle in your feet relaxing.

That beautiful energy of tranquility, peace, and love moves up your legs, into your ankles, your calves, your knees, your thighs; and you feel every muscle in your ankles, your calves, your knees, your thighs relaxing, relaxing, relaxing.

If you should hear any sound at all--a slamming door, a honking horn, a shouting voice--that sound will not disturb you. That sound will help you to relax even more.

Nothing will disturb you. Nothing will distress you in any way.

Now that beautiful energy of tranquility, peace, and love is moving up to your hips, your stomach, your back; and you feel every muscle in your hips, your stomach, your back relaxing...relaxing...relaxing.

With every breath that you take, you find that your body is becoming more and more relaxed.

Now the beautiful energy of tranquility, peace, and love enters your chest, your shoulders, your arms, even your fingers. You feel every muscle in your chest, your shoulders, your arms, and your fingers relaxing, relaxing, relaxing.

With every breath that you take, you find that you are becoming more and more relaxed.

Every part of your body is becoming free of tension. Every part of your body is becoming more and more relaxed.

Now that beautiful energy of tranquility, peace, and love moves into your neck, your face, the very top of your head. You feel every muscle in your neck, your face, and the very top of your head relaxing, relaxing, relaxing.

Your body is now relaxing, but your mind--your True Self --is very aware.

Now, a beautiful golden globe of light is moving toward you.

You are not afraid, for you realize--you *know*--that within this golden globe of light is your guide, one who has loved you since *before* you became you.

Feel the love as this intelligence comes closer to you. Feel the vibrations of love moving over you--warm, peaceful, tranquil.

You know that within this golden globe of light is one who has always loved you, just as you are.

You have been aware of this loving, guiding, presence ever since you were a child, a very small child.

You have been aware that this intelligence has always loved you unconditionally, just as you are--no facades, no masks, no pretenses

You feel love moving all around you. Two eyes are beginning to form in the midst of that golden light. The eyes of your guide! Feel the love flowing to you from your guide.

Now a face is forming. Oh, look at the smile on the lips of your guide. Feel the love that flows from your guide to you.

Now a body is forming. Behold the beauty of this form, structure, and stature of your guide. Feel the love that flows to you from the very presence of your guide, your guardian angel.

Your guide is now stretching forth a loving hand to you. Take that hand in yours. That's right. Lift up your hand and accept your guide's hand into yours. Feel that love flowing through you. Feel that love as you and your guide blend and flow together.

Now, hand in hand, you feel yourself being lifted higher and higher. Your guide is taking you to the dimension of spirit. You are moving higher, higher, higher.

You are moving into a higher vibration.

You are moving toward a place of higher awareness, of higher consciousness.

Now you have arrived in that place for which you have always yearned. Look around you. The trees, grass, sky, *everything* is more alive here. The colors are more vivid.

Look at yourself. You, too, have been transformed. It is as

if you have a new nervous system...new eyes, to see those things that you have never before seen...new ears to hear what you have never before heard.

Look at the people coming to greet you. Look at their eyes. Feel the love. You recognize so many of them.

Some you remember from your time beyond the stars.

Others are dear ones from the Earth plane who already have come home.

They reach out to touch you, to embrace you, to kiss you. You feel the love flowing all around you.

As you follow your guide through the Crystal City of Dreams, you feel love all around you. Love as you have never felt it on Earth. Love as you have yearned for it all of your life. You feel it now, all around you.

You may now ask your beloved guide any question that you wish. The wise one may answer in words, in a series of gestures, or by presenting a symbol. Watch closely and listen, for your guide is answering your question *now*.

(Pause at this point to permit the spiritual teaching to be received. If the answer to more than one question is desired, the above may be repeated. If a dialogue is established between you and your guide, permit it to continue as long as it is productive. When the contact begins to fade or when the desired information is received, come back to full consciousness in the following manner.)

Now you must return to full consciousness in the physical realm of Earth. Do not sorrow. Know that you may return to this Crystal City of Dreams again and again, as often as you wish. You are never separated from your guide on the spiritual vibration.

At the count of five you will be returned to full consciousness. **One**: coming awake. **Two**: coming more and more awake, moving the fingers, making a fist. **Three**: coming more and more awake, feeling very, very good in mind, body, and spirit. **Four**: coming awake, feeling better than you have felt in weeks and weeks, months and months. **Five**: fully awake. Feeling great! Filled with love and awareness!

Chapter 5

Understanding Dreams That Warn You

Can dreams actually warn us of dangers that lie ahead on life's pathway? There are those, of course, who consider anything gleaned from dreams to be pure coincidence or subconscious probings at best.

But we have documented cases of warning dreams and the accounts of men and women who have learned that not all dreams are symbolic. Some are very literal and should be heeded, as evidenced in the case of Gloria F.

A Dream of a Car Accident

Gloria F. could remember her dream in sharp detail the next morning when she awakened. Her boyfriend, Roger, had asked her to go riding with him across the Illinois state line into Indiana. As they drove along the highway, they had collided with another car, and both vehicles sustained great damage. Through drops of blood blurring her vision, Gloria had watched a plump woman with her arm bandaged and in a sling crawl out of the other car.

With the dream images firmly implanted in her mind, Gloria refused Roger's offer of an automobile ride on that beautiful Sunday afternoon.

"Come on," he coaxed. "Let's buzz over to Hammond and see if Indiana is as pretty as Illinois is today."

Gloria shook her head and told Roger about the dream that she had had the night before.

"Are you going to let a silly dream interfere with an outing on a day like today?" He laughed. "There won't be any wreck with old Steady Hand at the wheel. I'll even get you home early. Is it okay, Mrs. F?" he asked Gloria's mother, who was sitting on the porch swing reading the Sunday paper.

"I think an automobile ride would be pleasant on such a nice day," she answered, looking up from a recipe she was studying on the women's page. "Why don't you kids run along?"

Reluctantly, Gloria followed the triumphantly grinning Roger to his car. "Well, you drive carefully, Roger!"

Roger did drive carefully, a point he was to emphasize repeatedly, until, halfway between Gary and Hammond, Indiana, they crashed into another car.

Gloria's head went through the windshield, and she staggered from Roger's automobile, wiping the blood out of her eyes. Dimly, she saw the driver of the other car removing himself from behind the wheel with great effort. The driver's wife, a very plump woman, was tugging at him with one good arm. Her other arm was bandaged and in a sling.

"If I had only followed the warning in my dream instead of listening to Mom and Roger," Gloria kept saying to herself as she sat in the doctor's office waiting to have her skull stitched closed.

Dreams That Warn

The enigma of the precognitive dream has long fascinated humankind and has, from time to time, received scientific attention in "dream labs" established in various universities and hospitals.

It seems to us that some level of the unconscious mind may well be aware of the future and that it may occasionally flash a dramatic bit or scene to the conscious mind in a dream or trance, both of which are altered states of consciousness.

Psychical researcher H. F. Saltmarsh theorized that what we with our conscious level of mind term the "present moment" is not really a point of time, but a small interval called the "specious present." According to Saltmarsh's theory, our unconscious minds may be able to encompass a larger "specious present" than our conscious level of being. If, on occasion, some of this unconscious knowledge were to burst into the conscious, it might be interpreted as either a memory of a past event or a precognition of a future event.

We know that those events that we term our past are neatly catalogued somewhere in our unconscious. Some psychical researchers, such as Saltmarsh, believe that all events--past, present, and future--are part of the "present" and Eternal Now, for the deeper, transcendental level of the unconscious.

Studying the Telepathic Dream

The telepathic dream received a great deal of attention through the scientific inquiry of the Dream Laboratory at the Maimonides Medical Center in Brooklyn, New York. The experiments undertaken by the Dream Lab were designed to test the hypothesis that the altered state of consciousness associated with dreaming favors the appearance in the dream of a telepathically received stimulus. Eight experimental studies conducted by the laboratory between 1964 and 1969 produced five studies with statistically significant results.

In addition to the formal experimental studies, a number of pilot sessions were undertaken with equally rigid precautions against any kind of sensory leakage. Between March 25, 1964, and December 19, 1969, 83 pilot sessions involving one or more agents (senders) and a single sleeping subject (receiver) had been completed by the Dream Lab.

In a report prepared for the 1970 meeting of the Association for the Psychophysiological Study of Sleep in Santa Fe, New Mexico, Montague Ullman, Stanley Krippner, and Charles Honorton of the Maimonides Medical Center state:

> For these pilot sessions, judging of correspondences between the randomly selected target and dream content was accomplished by presenting outside judges with the entire target pool for that night and asking them to assign the rank of number one to that target picture that most closely resembled [the subject's] dreams and associational material. The other targets were also ranked on a similar basis. If the actual target was given a rank within the top

half of the distribution (e.g., number one or number two of the four-target pool), the rank was considered a "hit," supporting the telepathy hypothesis.

For the 83 pilot telepathy sessions completed by the end of 1969, the judges assigned 64 "hits" and 19 "misses." This distribution is statistically significant.... Of these 83 sessions, 11 were held with a relative (father, mother, spouse, sibling) serving as [agent], rather than a Dream Laboratory staff member. For these sessions there are nine "hits" and two "misses."

The Fire in the Wood Box

Consider the telepathic dream experienced by Mrs. G. D. of Wyoming.

Due to severe drought conditions in the ranch lands, Mrs. G.D. had taken a job in town in order to help out financially. During the summer she had commuted, but in the winter, because of the bad weather and the poor roads, Mrs. G.D. rented a small house in town while her husband and two sons stayed at the ranch.

At 3:00 A.M. on a January morning, the woman awakened with the acrid odor of burning cloth offending her nostrils. Terrified by the thought that her house might be on fire, she got out of bed and checked the small home thoroughly.

Although she found no fire in the house that she was renting, the feeling of danger persisted. She concluded that the fire must be in the house in which her husband and sons lay sleeping.

Mrs. G.D. called the ranch, but no one answered. She insisted that the operator keep trying. At last she heard the click of the receiver being lifted, and nearly simultaneously with his "Hello," she heard her older son coughing.

"Are you all right, Billie?" she shouted into the receiver.

"Mom! Mom! The house is full of smoke!"

Mrs. G.D. told her boy not to panic. "Go wake up Daddy and Jimmy. Find out where the smoke is coming from, put out the fire, and call me back!"

After an excruciatingly long 30 minutes, Mr. D. called his wife. The boys had placed their gloves on the wood box to dry out that evening when they came in from chores. Sometime during the night a spark had popped out of the stove and had landed on one of the gloves. The gloves had smoldered until they burst into flame. When they located the fire, the gloves had been completely burned, and the wood in the box was just beginning to crackle into flame.

Mrs. G.D. went back to bed, relieved that no real damage had been done to their ranch home.

"But I know that if I had not had that strange dream and smelled smoke where there was none and called the ranch, my home would have burned to the ground with my three loved ones in it," she stated in her account of the telepathic dream.

Shot By a Thief

Sometimes it appears that a telepathic bond between a man and a woman is so strong that they can share dreams. Numerous couples report having had common dreams or having been able to awake with an awareness of what the other had been experiencing in the dream state.

Mrs. C.H.C. dreamed that she died, and it may have been only the intervention of her husband, who was having a similar dream, which prevented her dream from coming true.

"I dreamed that I had been shot by a thief as I walked on the street," Mrs. C.H.C. said in her account of the strange dream. "Police officers came running up, and they, in turn, shot the criminal, but all that was too late to do me any good. They stretched my body out on a park bench, and I suddenly found myself walking through unfamiliar hilly and barren country.

"I walked on and on, watching the light fade and the countryside grow darker. Deep blackness was closing in around me, when I heard my husband shouting in my ear, `Honey! Honey! Don't leave me!' I heard his words over and over again, like a needle stuck in the groove of a phonograph record.

"I wanted to move, yet I could not. I wanted to answer him, but no sound came from my throat. I no longer had any control over my body. Dimly, I became aware of my husband sitting up in bed, turning me over on my back. I felt just a trickle of life returning to my body.

"I found myself awake, my sleeping husband bent over me. I managed to pat his hand, and he settled back down in bed with a deep sigh. Through all of his exertions, he had never awakened.

"I lay there for quite some time, cautiously trying all my loggy body parts to see if they were all working once again. At last I drifted back into an uneasy sleep.

"When the alarm went off the next morning, I awakened to find my husband holding me close to him. He told me that he had dreamed that I was leaving him forever to walk into a strange, barren land. He could not follow me past a barrier, but he could stand at the border and call for me to return."

Mrs. C.H.C. told her husband of her dream of death, and they lay there for several minutes marveling over the strange manner in that the dream states had been shared. Mr. C. raised himself on his elbow, started to speak, then stopped, a ghastly pallor draining his features of their normally ruddy hue. He reached to the bedside table and handed his wife a mirror.

"One look shocked me," Mrs. C.H.C. stated. "The skin under my eyes, around my mouth, and at the edge of my nostrils was blue. It felt cold and lifeless. My fingernails were blue, and so were my toenails and the palms of my hands. My whole body was still rather unmanageable. My husband noticed a place in my eye where the white seemed to have congealed.

"The blue left my fingernails and my palms, and I regained the use of my body after a few hours, but it took a week for the blue on my face to go away. I still have the spot in my eye. Once when a doctor saw it, he said that I must have been very close to death at some time for such a spot to have formed."

Dreams of Death May Herald Disease

Dr. Robert C. Smith of Michigan State University has found that some dreams of death or disruption of personal relationships may herald a serious illness. These dreams may manifest long before the extent of the disease becomes apparent to the dreamer or to his doctor.

As reported in the April 1989 issue of *Psychology Today*, Dr. Smith studied the dreams of 48 men and women who had been admitted to the hospital for cardiology tests. Although some of the patients had a history of chest pains or abnormal electrocardiograms, not one of them actually had been admitted because of a heart attack or any other acute heart problem.

Before their diagnostic testing, Smith had each patient recount a dream from the preceding year. When he compared dreams of separation or death with the patient, he found that the weaker the patient's heart, the more troubled were his or her dreams.

Heart disease manifested differently in the dreams of women and men. Men with weak or failing hearts had dreams rich with reference to death. Women in similar health states were more likely to dream of relationships being torn apart by forces beyond their control.

Smith readily points out that only about five percent of the patients who had death and separation dreams were suffering from serious physical illnesses. Most often the troubled dreams were prompted by psychological illness or extreme stress. However, such dreams could serve as significant warnings before an illness sets in, thereby providing one with time to prepare for the seige or to fend it off altogether. This is another good reason to learn to pay close attention to our dream scenarios.

Troubled Dreams of Pregnant Women

It has long been known that women gain a certain psychic ability during pregnancy, so it is logical that they would increase the number of dreams during this time--or at least increase their ability to recall their dreams. The many physical changes that take place during the months of pregnancy are directly related to the mental and psychic levels of awareness.

Many of the dreams experienced by women during this time concern fear for the baby's welfare or that the child will not be normal. Most of these, fortunately, are unfounded in reality.

Dr. Stanley Krippner, who served as the director of the William C. Menninger Dream Laboratory at Maimonides Medical Center in Brooklyn, New York, once told us:

> We found that a large percentage of pregnant women
> dreamed about giving birth to deformed babies and mon-

sters. These dreams express a natural fear that something will go wrong with the unborn child. So many mothers have these dreams that we do not consider them to be pathological in most cases.

In research conducted by Dr. Diane R. Schneider, with the cosponsorship of Dr. William Pomcranre, director of the Maimonides Hospital obstetrics department, it was determined that pregnancy, the wish for pregnancy, and the fear of pregnancy actually influence dream content to a high degree.

Nightmares of a Deformed Baby

Dr. R. L. Van de Castle, research consultant to Dr. Schneider's project, noted that, occasionally, a woman may have a dream that accurately foresees the future in regard to her pregnancy and delivery. Dr. Van de Castle discovered one woman who claimed that she had recurring nightmares for several years, ever since the time she had seen illustrations of an abnormal fetus in her fiance's medical textbook.

The woman said that her dreams always were identical. She lay in a hospital bed in hard labor. Her sister was always in her dream, and she, too, was about to give birth. The dream always ended the same way. Her sister would produce a healthy, normal child, and the dreamer, after a long, excruciating labor, would bear a deformed baby.

The woman suffered through the dreams for nearly six years before she married and became pregnant for the first time.

"Then I knew instinctively and absolutely that the pregnancy would repeat itself identically with the dream," she told Dr. Van de Castle. "And it did, even to my sister actually being pregnant at the same time that I was."

As in the recurring dream, the woman's sister gave birth to a healthy, normal girl, while she bore a deformed, stillborn child.

When the woman became pregnant again a year later, her doctor warned her to expect a psychologically difficult pregnancy because of her previous experience.

"But I assured him that now the dream had lived itself out

in reality, there would be no more worry on my part," the woman said. "The dream never recurred, and I gave birth to a normal child."

An Angel Saved the Unborn Child

Mrs. M.J.'s precognitive dream had a happier message, and because the young woman believed in its declaration, she saved the life of her unborn child.

Mrs. M.J. was in her second month of pregnancy when her doctor advised her that she must have an abortion. In his opinion, it would be fatal for her to bear the child. At her husband's urging, the woman made the necessary arrangements to be aborted legally.

Then, the night before the operation, she had a dream in which an angel appeared before her, holding a handsome baby boy in his arms. On the strength of that dream, Mrs. M. J. refused the abortion and gave birth to the smiling baby boy she had seen so vividly in her dream.

A Lovely Little Girl in a Lovely Garden

When Mrs. E.R. was pregnant, she and her husband lived with in-laws, and she charitably described their arrangement as "an unhappy situation."

Whenever she had a particularly trying day, Mrs. E.R. would experience the same beautiful dream in which she was walking among lovely flowers with a little girl at her side and soothing, uplifting music playing in the background.

After her little girl was born and they had moved into their own home , the beautiful dream ceased, but Mrs. E.R. often thought of it.

When her daughter was about five, Mrs. E.R. took the girl along to a flower show that was being held at a convention hall in a nearby city. The entire hall had been transformed into a lovely, fragrant garden, and an orchestra played soothing, uplifting music.

"Suddenly it struck me," Mrs. E.R. wrote in her report of the paranormal experience. "This was my dream, that beautiful, tension-relieving dream that I had when I was pregnant!"

The most remarkable facet of this particular report occurred when her daughter tugged at Mrs. E.R.'s skirt, her eyes sparkling excitedly, and said, "We've been here lots and lots of times before, haven't we, Mommy?"

Psychologists have only begun to explore the many subtle, unconscious links that exist between the expectant mother and the child she nurtures in her womb.

A Checklist for Your "Warning Dreams"

Thankfully, every time that we have awful dreams about terrible things happening to our loved ones and friends the dreams do not prove to be precognitive warnings. Many of these very uncomfortable dreams are due to natural feelings of anxiety. Because our loved ones are so precious to us, it would be the worse kind of reality if something bad happened to them, so we more or less exorcise the demons of fear by enacting dream scenarios that permit us to release negative apprehensions.

While it often is difficult at times to distinguish between a dream intended to warn and a dream intended to release anxiety, such a checklist as the following may prove helpful in permitting you to make a more careful analysis of the nocturnal drama that you have witnessed.

What was the locale of the dream?_____

Were you in a familiar setting or did the environment constitute more of a fantasy locale? _____

At what time of day did the dream scenario occur? _____
_____

At what season of the year did the drama take place? _____
_____

What was the condition of the weather? _____
_____

Jot down what it was about the setting of the dream that made it seem to real to you. _____

_____

Were you observing the action of the dream or were you an active participant in the drama? _____

_____

What were your physical circumstances in the dream? Were you feeling well or ill? _____
Were you calm or upset? _____

Do you feel that you behaved in a manner that would be typical of your likely responses if the event had been "real" and not a dream drama or did you conduct yourself in a manner that you would adjudge as strange or peculiar? _____

_____

Jot down any aspects of your behavior in the dream scenario that you would consider untypical behavior on your part. _____

_____
_____
_____

Who were the other characters in the dream? _____

_____

If all of the characters were known to you, did they all behave in a characteristic manner? _____

Make note of any particular elements of behavior that may have seemed foreign to any of the participants. _____

_____

If all of the characters were familiar to you, did they all dress in a style that seemed appropriate to their usual mode of dress?

_____

Make a note of any item of dress that seemed inappropriate to your knowledge of the actors in the dream. _____

_____

Remember any elements of conversation in the dream. Did all of the dream actors speak in patterns typical of their normal speech styles? _____

If any one or more of them seemed to employ language unchar-acteristic of what you would consider to be the typical speech style of that person or persons, make a note of what was said that seemed to you to be inappropriate. _____

_____

_____

Review the dream carefully for any puns or tricks of language that might have been employed. _____

_____

Remember now the tragedy or the terrible event of that the dream seemed to present a warning. _____

_____

Did the event itself seem real or did it seem too fantastic to ever occur in Earth-plane actuality? _____

_____

Did the event seem to be occurring in the "now" as you observed it? _____

Remember your emotions as you witnessed the event. _____

_____

What were your honest thoughts as you beheld the situation? No matter how terrible the event, did one level of your psyche assess the situation as something that the participants (perhaps yourself included) had brought upon themselves? _____

_____

Was the episode something that you had been fearful might actually happen in earth plane reality? _____

_____

Was there any sense that "justice" had been done? _____

Even though you truly do not wish such an event to occur, as you witnessed the dream situation, did you feel deep within you that you have predicted such a terrible occurrence, that you really knew that the tragedy would some day be liable to occur? _____

_____

Sit quietly for several minutes and reflect upon the "plot" of the dream scenario. Could the ostensible warning of a terrible event to come be symbolic of changes within the lives of the participants? For example, a death scene can sometimes be symbolic of a new beginning, a rebirth.

Check the dream dictionary in this book for other possible symbolic interpretations of objects and events in your dream. After you have done this, write down all the possible symbols that you can see might have been contained within your dream. ____

_____
_____
_____
_____
_____
_____

Now that you have completed this checklist, write below your honest assessment of whether or not the dream truly contained a precognitive warning. _____

_____

If your answer is yes, then you must proceed with utmost caution. You cannot simply contact the other people involved and scream out your alleged prophetic warnings.

You must respect free will, karma, and individual responsibility. At the same time, you must never stray from the possibility that you may be incorrect in your assessment of your dream's predictive power.

Pray. Meditate. If you remain compelled to speak to the others and if you feel that it is your responsibility to warn them of the possibility of your dream coming true, then present the dream scenario to them in a very low-key manner. Share it with them as a personal experience and permit them to make up their own minds about the situation.

On the other side of the coin, you may be correct. It may, indeed, be your responsibility to warn them about the events in your dream. Your dream may be as true and actual a warning of the future as the dreams of those men and women whose case histories were presented in this chapter.

Chapter 6

Use Your Dreams
to Solve Problems

On the day before Easter in 1920, Dr. Otto Loewi, who was for many years research pharmacologist at the New York University College of Medicine, had gone to bed, hoping to awaken to a cheerful Easter morning.

But in the middle of the night he had a very strange dream, and he awoke to record its details as quickly as possible. He scribbled furiously on a pad of paper at his bedside, then put the pencil down and fell back to sleep until dawn.

Dr. Loewi awoke convinced that he had dreamed something very important, but when he turned to the notes he had written the night before, he found them completely undecipherable. Disappointed and curious about the content of his dream, Dr. Loewi wondered about it for the entire day.

As early as 1903 a very thorny problem in the field had come to Dr. Loewi's attention. The study of the function and the mechanism of the nerves in the human body was in its embryo stage at the time, and the most widely accepted theory was that the nerves of the body stimulated the muscles by transmitting a wave along with the minute electrical impulse that traveled the length of the nerve fiber.

At the time this theory was practically not testable, and for many reasons Dr. Loewi could not be satisfied with it. He discussed a different prospect with his colleagues.

He proposed that chemical changes in the muscle were responsible for the body's reaction to stimuli, arguing that minute amounts of chemicals were released from the nerve fibers themselves, and that these chemicals caused the expansion and contraction of the muscles. To Dr. Loewi and even to some of his colleagues, this theory seemed more plausible than the other, but, like the other, there seemed no possible way to test it.

The theory was pushed into Dr. Loewi's subconscious as other considerations came to his attention.

All through Easter day in 1920, Dr. Loewi pondered his strange dream.

At 3:00 A.M. the next morning, he experienced the same dream. The dream gave the details of an experiment that would allow him to test the hypothesis that he had discarded 17 years before.

Taking no chances that he might forget the dream again, Dr. Loewi arose and hurried to his laboratory. Had he thought of an idea in broad daylight, Loewi might have discarded it immediately as unworkable, but while under the compelling influence of the dream, he hurriedly prepared for the experiment.

Then, as now, the creature most widely used in the study of the nervous system was the frog. The experiment outlined in the dream called for the use of two properly prepared frog hearts kept alive in a Ringer solution--a substance resembling blood plasma.

The experiment was very simple. A particular nerve called the vagus nerve was stimulated in one of the frog hearts, then the Ringer solution was transferred to the other container. The vagus nerve of the heart in the second container had been carefully dissected away so there was no chance that it could be accidentally stimulated.

The result of the experiment was that the second heart reacted as if the vagus nerve had not been dissected away, showing that it was indeed a chemical change that triggered muscular response and not an electronic wave from the nerve.

This experiment forced an abrupt change in the theory of muscle stimulation and triggered a series of independent experiments--not only verifying Dr. Loewi's result but going further. The chemical that induced this particular change in the ʰ of the frog was positively identified as acetylcl first been isolated by H. H. Dale, Dr. Loewi's clo. Together these men shared the Nobel Prize for medicine in 1936.

Although the experiment itself had a striking effect on the academic world of physiology, the manner in which the idea for the test came to Dr. Loewi is perhaps even more astounding. It is conceivable that ideas could be transferred from one mind to another during sleep. But when such ideas are not in the mind of man, from where could they possibly arise?

Before his death in 1961, Dr. Loewi stated that he could not possibly answer this question. Perhaps no man can, but it is certain that Dr. Loewi's dream provided the key to subsequent research that eventually gained him the Nobel Prize.

Solving Problems in Dreams

Solving problems via the dream state is as old as man himself. Edison, it is said, had the habit of curling up in his rolltop desk to catch brief naps that sometimes constituted his entire sleep schedule. After such a nap he would emerge with the answers to problems that had plagued him during his waking state.

Elias Howe failed at the conscious level to perfect a workable sewing machine. Then one night he dreamed that a savage king ordered him to invent a sewing machine, and when he was unable to comply, the spear-armed natives raised their weapons to kill him. At that exact moment, he noticed that each spear had a hole in it just above the point. This vision gave him the much-needed clue to the commercial perfection of the sewing machine.

A famous scientist who used his dreams to solve problems was Niels Bohr. One night Bohr dreamed of a sun composed of burning gas with planets spinning around it, attached by thin threads. He realized that this explained the structure of the atom, which eventually led to the field of atomic physics and, ultimately, atomic energy.

Wordsworth credited dreams for the many poems he wrote. "Kubla Khan" was the result of a dream by Coleridge. Jules Verne's monsters of *Twenty Thousand Leagues Under the Sea* certainly smack of Jungian archetypal characters, and the classic *Jane Eyre* was spun from the dreams of Charlotte Brontë.

Obviously, not all of us are inventors, scientists, or writers destined for lasting fame, but there is absolutely no reason why we cannot benefit just as much from our dreams by using them to solve our problems and to find hidden reservoirs of creativity in our subconscious.

"Before going to sleep," Roy Eugene Davis advises,

> ask the subconscious level of mind to bring forth solutions to problems and answers to questions. The answers will happen, either in a dream or in the middle of the night or when one awakens in the morning.
>
> Also, while asking the subconscious for aid, expect the superconscious level of mind to filter down from the soul level the needed data--if it is not already filed in the subconscious level.

A Technique for Meaningful Dreaming

"This basic technique is simplicity itself," says Al G. Manning, author and ESP researcher. "It requires a small piece of Scotch tape--or surgical tape if you prefer--and either the person's favorite meditation stone, or perhaps a paper clip--any small object that can easily be taped to the forehead."

Next, Manning says, sit quietly in front of the mirror the last thing before going to bed and, somewhat ceremoniously, tape either the stone or the paper clip to the center of the forehead in the area that is called the Brow Chakra or brow center.

As you're doing this, look at your face in the mirror, regarding it as if it were your own subconscious mind, and simply state: "This is your reminder that during the course of the evening sleep, you are to wake me when I have had a meaningful dream, just long enough to make enough notes to remember in the morning, and then put me back into a rich and relaxing sleep."

Of course, it then requires pencil and paper, and perhaps a small nightlight by the side of the bed that can be turned on in such a way that it does not hurt the eyes. Go back now and double-underline the instructions: "Wake me when I have had a *meaningful* dream."

In his own experience, Manning says

> When I began this process, I said, "Wake me every time I have a dream." And so the first night I recorded

six dreams; the second night, about 12; the third night about 24; and the fourth night about 40--at which point I said, "The hell with it! I've got more material than I can analyze in the next six months! Let's stop there for a while!"

You must wake up and record the dream in order to be able to remember it in the morning. No matter how vivid it is, if you don't make the notes, by morning it just slips quickly away.

Manning suggests a variation that he has used quite successfully. When you're working on a particular problem, change the programming by writing on a very small piece of paper the question you would like resolved in the dream state. Put this behind the meditation stone on the forehead, so it is close to the forehead.

The instruction is: "This is your reminder to bring me a dream in answer to this question, positively, and as clear as possible. You will wake me to record this dream answer."

The ability to generate the basic idea of waking up after a dream to write it down should be fairly well established before one tries the variation. The reason for this is because when you have asked something specific, you may be asking in the area of an emotional block so that there would be a tendency for the subconscious to ignore the request or to bring you an aberration.

If you have not had earlier successes, there would be a tendency to become very discouraged when there were no apparent results the first night. We all recognize that the more important we think a problem is, the more difficult it is to get good, quick answers. It may take two or three blank nights before you get anything; if it's a serious problem, you have to get past the point of demanding the instantaneous thing. Keep at it until you get results, even if it takes up to eight days.

In his view, Manning's research has indicated the following:

* The dream state can be a good place for dialogue with your own subconscious or unconscious being.

* No matter how vivid a dream is, it must be recorded at the time. You must be programmed to wake up and record it if you're going to be able to remember enough detail for it to be useful.

* Programming to answer specific questions is quite rea-

sonable and proper and can be highly effective.

* You must distinguish between the unimportant dream state, wherein you are simply a spectator of strange things on the astral plane.

* When you do touch the prophetic state, recognize the challenge aspect; do not blindly accept or capitulate to Fate. Make the outcome as positive as one would dare hope--or perhaps more so with some good effort.

Discover Your Personal Sacred Moment

It has been said by those who devote their lives to studying such subjects as anthropology, mythology, and religion that all ritual observances have a long and faraway beginning time, a sacred event to which a culture can trace its origins. A familiar illustration to those of us in the Judeo-Christian tradition would be the story of Adam and Eve and the Tree of Knowledge. For centuries we have traced the creation of our humanity, our species consciousness, and our world to that mythical event.

Each of us has his or her own personal myth of "the beginning," of a time to which we might return in our individual sacred moment and our unique ritualized measurement of reality.

Brad has shared his mythical beginning when, as a small boy on an Iowa farm, he sat in the midst of a clump of lilac bushes and perceived the world from that sacred vantage point.

Now, even as an adult in his 50s, whenever Brad needs help in rescuing his center from the insults of the material world, he goes back in his memory to that special, magic place--his mythical moment of the beginning. Brad mentally returns to that place in the lilac bushes when he needs a fortress against the stresses and pressures of the real world. It is from this eternally safe and protected vantage spot that he can regroup his energies, shore up his psyche, and resume the Quest with renewed strength.

Each of you has a similar magic, mythical place--a sacred spot to which you retreated as a child and felt secure and protected against the fears and awful awareness of a reality external to you and to your inner spark of divinity.

In learning to utilize your dreams to solve your problems, first practice lying in bed and trying to remember your individual magic place just before you fall asleep.

Once you have truly *remembered* with all of your senses what your mythical place of personal origin looked like, smelled like, felt like; once you have heard any sounds that were around you there and recalled any tastes somehow associated with that time; then you are ready to pull in the power of your internal myth and use it to solve those problems that are the most troublesome to you at home, school, work, in your personal relationships, and in your career.

Use any of the relaxation techniques in this book to place yourself in a receptive attitude. Remember that these visualizations are very much like rehearsals for your significant dreams when you truly are asleep.

As before, you may read the relaxation technique aloud, and pause now and then to allow its energy to permeate your true essence. You may do the same with the visualization exercise. Or, as previously suggested, you may have a friend or family member read both the relaxation process and the visualization to you. Others, as we have pointed out, prefer recording their own voice, reading these exercises and playing the tape back as your own guide to expanding awareness.

After you have placed yourself in a state of deep and peaceful relaxation through one of the processes suggested above, permit the Wise Alchemist to help you solve your problem.

Visiting a Spiritual Alchemist of Old to Solve Your Problems

Now that you are totally and completely relaxed, visualize the color of blue moving over your body as if it were a blanketlike aura. Feel it moving over your legs, relaxing them even more. Feel it moving over your stomach, your chest, your arms, your neck--soothing them, relaxing your body even more, even more.

Now as you make a hood of the blue-colored auric cover, feel the color of blue permeating your psyche so that it is totally activating your abilities to understand the teachings that you are about to receive from the wise Spiritual Alchemist.

You are very receptive, very aware. You feel very much attuned with Higher Consciousness. You are prepared now to go deep, deep within...deep, deep within....

You are seeing memory patterns before you. They may be your memories of other dreams, other life experiences, other past life awarenesses. It does not matter. It does not matter even if you are perceiving the memories of another.

What does matter is that these memories are taking you to a faraway time, and you are moving back on the vibration of the Eternal Now.

You often have heard of the ancient alchemists, those scholars who sought to turn base metals into gold. You are moving back in time to meet a great Spiritual Alchemist, one who had the ability to turn the baseness of troublesome problems into the gold of meaningful solutions.

This wise one can hear the worst of troubles and transform them into the best of opportunities.

As you move back in Time, you are hearing the words of another great alchemist, the physician known as Paracelsus.

He is saying that it is humankind that must fulfill Nature. God did not create objects made of iron. God created the metal that mortals must enjoin with fire in order to fashion useful items.

Everything is first created in its primary state. It is the alchemist who must summon the fire of creativity to transform the impure into the pure.

Alchemy is the art that can separate the useful from the useless and transmute it into its final substance and its ultimate essence.

Only the Soul lives eternally. Just as a seed must rot if it is to bear fruit, the Soul endures while the body decays.

Decay is the midwife of great things. It brings about the birth and rebirth of forms a thousand times improved. This is the highest and greatest mystery of God.

There is nothing in Heaven or in Earth that is not also in humankind. In you is God, who is also in Heaven. Likewise, all the forces of Heaven operate in you.

In you is the innate ability to practice all arts, all crafts, all sciences, all skills. But not all of your awarenesses have yet been awakened. Those things that are to become manifest within you first must be awakened.

All potentialities are inherent within you, but only those that are awakened will come forth.

It is in sleep, in dreams, that the greatest of awakenings can occur.

Your inner awareness is telling you now that you will soon meet the wise Spiritual Alchemist in a secret room beneath the Great Pyramid of Giza.

You have the knowledge that for centuries certain worthy supplicants have received a mystical transfer of knowledge and wisdom in hidden rooms in the pyramids.

You are aware that great energies, incredible powers are focused through the pyramids.

See yourself now walking a street in ancient Egypt. There is a full Moon, and you can see everything around you very clearly.

You are approaching a home with a courtyard. It is the home of the Spiritual Alchemist.

It is here that you will meet with other adepts and be led to a secret room beneath the Great Pyramid. It is in this secret room that you will receive the answer to the problem that so perplexes you.

Take a moment to realize fully your emotions as you walk up the path to the Spiritual Alchemist's home. Take a moment to understand fully the nature of the problem that you wish to overcome.

Look at the home of the Spiritual Alchemist. What plants grow near the walls? What is there about the immediate area that most captures your attention?

Now you are at the door of the home. Be aware of your inner thoughts and feelings as you knock. Feel your knuckles strike the wooden planks.

One of the Spiritual Alchemist's disciples opens the door. Become totally aware of this person. Observe clothing, body shape, face, eyes, mouth, the way the hands are held. Look into the eyes of this disciple and see and understand clearly if you know this person on some level of awareness.

The disciple gestures that you should enter, and as you walk into the home you see the crackling flames of a great open fireplace. A man dressed in robes sits near the fire, stirring a large iron kettle with a wooden ladle. You know that it is the Spiritual Alchemist.

As he turns to face you, you see his features clearly. Become totally aware of him. See his clothes, body, face, eyes, mouth, the way he holds his hands.

He indicates that you should be seated. He hands you a cup of his favorite herbal tea.

Accept it. Savor the tea in your mouth. Taste it completely. It is a special tea, and you will remember its taste.

You have brought a present for the Spiritual Alchemist so that he will recognize you as a seeker of wisdom, as one who truly wishes to solve life's problems in a reasoned manner.

Take your present out of the leather bag in which you have carried it. See what it is that you hand the alchemist. See his reactions.

The Spiritual Alchemist rises and gestures that you and the other waiting supplicants should follow him.

As you rise, become aware of the others who have come to seek answers to their problems. Become aware if there are any supplicants whom you may recognize.

Look at their eyes, mouths, and body shapes. If it is for your good and your gaining, you will recognize those whom you should know. Look closely at their eyes, and if it is to be, you will remember them.

The Spiritual Alchemist pushes aside a curtain and steps into an open doorway. Follow him.

Now you are in a tunnel. You know that you are being led to a secret room beneath the Great Pyramid. You know that you are walking in a tunnel that leads from the Spiritual Alchemist's home to the secret room.

Experience fully your emotions as you walk silently through the tunnel. See torches set into the walls. Be aware of any smells, any sounds.

Now you stand in a great room. Look around slowly. There are statues. There are paintings. There are hieroglyphs and symbols etched on the walls.

Experience fully the range of objects and symbols in this room. Remember them.

The Spiritual Alchemist beckons to you. He is showing you a great crystal that is supported on a golden tripod. He says that it is the Philosopher's Stone. He tells you that it will aid in achieving a transmutation of your base problems into golden solutions.

As you stare into the great crystal, the Spiritual Alchemist tells you that you will see the answer to your problem reveal itself in one of the facets of the stone's shining surface.

He says that the answer that you see will be personal, completely customized for your particular needs. Whatever knowledge and solution you perceive will be completely for your good and your gaining.

Look deeply into the crystal. Begin to perceive images, objects, symbols, information...knowledge for your good and your gaining...an answer that will solve your problem.

Your personal answer is manifesting **now**!

(At this point, there should be a pause of at least 60 seconds for the complete manifestation of the solution to your problem. After that pause, slowly begin to count back as provided in any of the previous exercises and techniques in this book. Feelings of well-being, peace of mind, a positive attitude, and a sense of accomplishment should be emphasized as you count back.)

Chapter 7

Out-of-Body Projections During Dreams

When one has a vivid dream of his loved ones and his home when he is traveling and separated from family and hearth, is that person simply dreaming of being home--or has his mind-spirit, his Essential Self, actually projected to his longed-for environs?

Our research has lead us to identify the following types of out-of-body experiences--or, one might say, situations in which OBEs might occur:

1. Projections that occur while the subject sleeps.

2. Projections that occur while the subject is undergoing surgery, childbirth, tooth extraction, etc.

3. Projections that occur at the time of accident, during which the subject suffers a violent physical jolt that seems, literally, to catapult his spirit from his physical body.

4. Projections that occur during intense physical pain.

5. Projections that occur during acute illness.

6. Projections that occur during pseudodeath, wherein the subject is revived and returned to life through heart massage or other medical means.

7. Projections that occur at the moment of physical death when the deceased subject appears to a living percipient with whom he has had a close emotional link.

In addition to these spontaneous, involuntary experiences, there also seem to be those voluntary and conscious projections during which the subject deliberately endeavors to free his Essential Self from his physical body.

Out-of Body Projections Are Not Uncommon

Some years ago, Dr. Eugene E. Bernard told Thomas Leach of the *Chicago American Magazine* that on the basis of his preliminary research, he would estimate that one out of every hundred persons has experienced some sort of out-of-body projection.

Dr. Bernard stated that his study indicated that such projections occurred most often "...during time of stress; during natural childbirth; during minor surgery; and at times of extreme fear."

In addition to these spontaneous instances, Dr. Bernard admitted that he also had encountered a number of "old pros" who seemed to be able to have out-of-body projections almost at will.

Decades ago, the great psychical researcher Frederic W. H. Myers believed out-of-body experiences to be the most extraordinary achievement of the human will.

> What can be a more central action--more manifestly the outcome of whatsoever is deepest and most unitary in man's whole being? Of all vital phenomena, I say, this is the most significant; this self-projection is the one definite act that it seems as though a man might perform equally well before and after bodily death.

Dr. Hornel Hart's investigation of out-of-body experiences and "psi" phenomena led him to theorize that the brain was but an instrument by which consciousness expresses itself, rather than a generator that produces consciousness. Dr. Hart contended that the available evidence strongly supported the testimonies of those individuals who maintain that the essence of personal consciousness might observe and act at long distances away from the brain.

To primitive man a dream was an actual experience enacted by the soul as it wandered about during sleep. Today we still do not know a great deal about the mysteries of sleep and dreams, but electroencephalograph records of brain waves and the study of rapid-eye-movement patterns have convinced psychologists and dream scientists that the action of a dream (for most people) takes place within the individual dream machinery and is confined within the labyrinth of the brain.

Philosophically, it may be fine to argue that when one glimpses the Taj Mahal in a dream he is in reality having an out-of-body experience and actually seeing the beautiful white monument; but unless one can in some way substantiate the mind-trip, such an experience will remain classified as a dream to all but the most credulous.

For some who have accomplished OBE, a meaningful subjective proof exists that allows them to believe that their experience was indeed a genuine one. Others are able to substantiate their projections with objective proof or the testimonies of witnesses.

The Soldier Who Dreamed Himself Home

When he was called into service on September 5, 1917, Milton C. Watson was like so many young doughboys of World War I. He never before had been away from home for more than a night or two and was terribly homesick, he wrote in an article in the September 1967 issue of *Fate* magazine.

On April 13, 1918, his company boarded a train for Camp Upton, New York, and prepared to sail to England. When he had been in Romsey, England, for 13 days and still had not had any mail from home catch up with him, Watson remembers, his homesickness reached a most painful level. It was just before his company was transferred to Southhampton to sail for France that Milton Watson had the most peculiar dream of his life.

He dreamed that he left the tent in which he was quartered, went to Romsey, caught a train for Liverpool, then boarded a ship for New York.

Step by step the strange dream traced the actual course that Watson would take if he actually were going home. He could see himself stowing away behind some large trunks in the hold of the ship. After the vessel docked in New York, he watched himself buy a train ticket at the Pennsylvania Station.

No one was there to meet him when he got off the train at the home depot, but he walked the quarter mile down the dirt road that took him directly to his parents' front gate.

In his dream he lifted the noisy latch, closed the gate, walked up on the front porch, and opened the door. He looked around, saw that everything at home was just the way he had left it...then the sound of the bugle woke him up.

When he wrote to his sister to tell her of his strange dream, he received a most amazing reply:

> ...she said that my brother Perry and my nephew Charles Evans, sleeping in my old bedroom, both had hopped out of bed the night of the dream, rushed into the front room and told the family I was home. They said they had heard me open the gate and enter the house. The folks had a hard time convincing them I was not there.

Keeping an Eye on the Employees While Asleep

In one of his earlier books, *The Mind Travellers*, Brad relates the following account.

> R.R. of Alaska runs a butcher shop and maintains his living quarters above his place of business. One afternoon he suffered an onslaught of influenza and decided to take a couple of aspirins and go to bed for the day. He left a young employee, T.G., in charge and went upstairs to lie down.
>
> "I had not lain there long," R.R. recalled, "when I lapsed into a kind of feverish sleep. I had taken the aspirin, but I knew that my fever was pretty high. My wife was downtown shopping, and I wished that she would hurry and get home.
>
> "I would drift off to sleep, then wake up, then drift off again. The next thing I knew, I seemed to slide right out of my body. I thought it was some kind of weird dream, and I felt kind of nonchalant about the whole thing. I remembered thinking that I could slide right though the wall if I wanted to--and sure enough, I did.
>
> "I slipped right down to the butcher shop, and I saw T.G. eating an uncooked wiener from the meat case. This was a bad habit of his, and I had got after him many times about this.
>
> "One of his friends was in the shop, and he asked T.G. if the boss wouldn't get sore if he knew T.G. was eating wieners again. 'Ah, he's upstairs sleeping,' I heard

T.G. reply. 'What he won't know won't hurt him.' Then he offered his friend a wiener and they both ate two or three more.

"I wished that my wife would come walking in on them and give them what-for. The moment I thought of M., I was standing beside her in an ice-cream shop. M. was eating a big chocolate sundae heaped with nuts. I thought, 'Oh, baby, is this how you keep on your diet? You'll come home tonight and barely eat anything and I'll praise you for sticking to your diet.'

"It was funny how everything I saw related to food, and even though I knew I couldn't really feel anything because I was passing through walls and people, I started getting kind of nauseous. I looked at M. scooping in that sundae and I got sicker. Then I had an image of T. G. stuffing an uncooked wiener into his mouth and I got sicker still.

"Everything started spinning around and rushing past, and I seemed to land on my bed with a thump. I got to my feet and rushed to the bathroom, and later I felt quite a bit better. My fever was still plenty high, but I walked down to the butcher shop.

"When M. came home and found me lying sick in bed, she immediately set about fixing me some hot broth. 'You can join me,' I told her. 'It won't hurt you to skip a big meal after that big chocolate sundae you had downtown at K's.'

"I told my wife all about the experience, but I am certain she believed that one of my friends saw her shopping and tattled on her for eating the big sundae. But I know these experiences were real, and I feel I received proof enough to convince me that I wasn't just dreaming. Somehow, I was really there."

She Visited Her Sister's Home in a Dream

Helen Louise Utter is another who is convinced that she "was really there" at the scene of her dream (based on her report in *Fate*, December 1967).

When Helen Louise Utter was growing up in Wilkes-Barre, Pennsylvania, a financial tragedy resulting from a bad investment in a mine affected many of the city's residents, including her own family.

Her sister, Ann, 14 years her senior, moved out of Wilkes-Barre when her husband and his father decided to move to Idaho to start a hotel. Helen and her parents moved to Sayre, Pennsylvania, where she married Leon Utter; but after her father died and her mother left for France, Helen began to feel the separation from Ann and her seven nieces and nephews more acutely than ever before.

Then on that night in September 1913, when she was feeling particularly lonely, she had her most unusual dream.

She found herself in a strange city, walking up an alley off a main street. She saw a large barn and an old car up on blocks. A beautiful pine tree stood halfway down a path to a house. On one side of the path she saw lovely gardens of flowers; on the other, a lush vegetable garden.

She entered the house through a large enclosed porch. Helen walked into the kitchen and was shocked when she recognized Ann's Crown Vista china from England. She was in Ann's house!

In all of their correspondence, Ann had never described her home. Now Helen was getting a firsthand tour by means of a dream.

She carefully noted the floor plan of each room, taking delight when she would discover a familiar object, such as the tea wagon, one of grandmother's paintings, the Oriental sword and the hammered-brass pistols that had been the gift of a Chinese student whom Ann had taught in New York.

She looked up the staircase and knew that Ann, her husband, and their seven children lay asleep in their bedrooms.

When Helen awakened, she told her dream to Leon, who convinced her that, though vivid, the experience could only have been a dream and nothing more.

A few years later, Helen had her first baby; and when the child was just three months old, Leon became seriously ill. Physicians advised the Utters to move to a different climate, and Helen's sister insisted that they try Idaho. On May 30, 1916, they began the train trip to Sandpoint.

When they were at last met at the station by Ann and her family, they all piled laughing and talking into their new Buick and turned off into an alley that led to their home. As they turned, Helen said to her husband: "Look! Remember my dream? There was the large barn. We turned and there sat the old Buick on its blocks, the pine tree, and gardens...."

She turned to her sister and told her that she had "been there before."

Helen went on: "I can tell you just how your house is planned and furnished, where the pictures hang. Is the table in the breakfast room set with the pink dishes from England?"

Helen Louise Utter states that her sister's house was precisely as she had seen it in her vivid "dream."

An After-Dinner Nap Took Her to the Future

As we have seen in the previous report by Mrs. Utter, a fairly common type of out-of-body experience during sleep has the agent projecting to a place that he or she will one day visit in his or her physical body.

A Mrs. W.N. of Georgia writes that she lay down one night to take a short nap after dinner and felt herself suddenly outside of her body. Thinking it only a very realistic kind of dream, Mrs. W. N. relaxed and allowed the "dream" to carry her consciousness along through the night sky.

Suddenly she was in a hotel room. "I knew that it was a hotel room the moment I 'landed' there," Mrs. W.N. writes. "It just had that feel to it."

> I took note of the furniture, the bedspread, and I read the rules for overnight guests tacked behind the door. The room had been freshly carpeted and appeared to be very modern, but I was surprised to see that it had an old-fashioned bathtub--one of those with legs shaped like claws gripping balls.
>
> I looked out the window and I could see a neon light flashing on and off to the right. It was advertising a milk product from a certain dairy.
>
> I was just beginning to feel a bit uneasy, like maybe

all this wasn't a dream, when I felt a strange sensation along the entire length of my body, as if something were pulling at me. I imagined that I felt very much like a nail being attracted by a magnet. There was a rapid rush of images, and I was back on my couch.

My husband and daughter were standing above me with strange smiles on their faces. They teased me about being such a sound sleeper. They had been trying to awaken me for several minutes without success.

About a month later, my sister-in-law was involved in an automobile accident, and I went to be with her, as my brother was in the service and was stationed overseas. I visited her at the hospital and promised her that I would stay for another two or three days until she was feeling better.

A nurse recommended a hotel, and when I checked into my room I was not at all surprised to find the room of my most unusual dream. The bathtub with the funny legs, the neon sign flashing off to the right, the furnishings --all things were just as I had seen them during my peculiar after-dinner nap.

The Eternal Now

Déja vu may not be the same as out-of-body experience, but it borders on the field of precognition. This phenomenon is not as rare as one might think, and for that matter, it probably occurs in the dream state more often than we might suspect. Without getting into such theories as time warp, it might be sufficient to say that by some strange means we at times are able to project mentally into the future and witness certain events that are far from our normal or conscious state at that particular time. Later, when we see that actual event begin to unfold, we have the feeling of having been there before--déja vu.

While an OBE seems to represent one's ability to slip out of the body and appear at some other point in the current time zone, the déja vu experience is related more to a mental mind-hopping into some future point in time. Yet, one of the basic thoughts in metaphysical circles is that there is, in reality, no such thing as "time" as we normally consider it. Yesterday, today, and tomorrow are all the same, so perhaps we are really practicing out-of-body travel in the "now," although by man's calculations of such matters it is to some distant point in time.

Projecting Images of the Physical Body

When Dr. Eugene Barnard speaks of "old pros" who can project at will, he is referring to such talented individuals as Olof Jonsson, the famous Swedish mystic.

"In the midst of parapsychological investigators, I have succeeded in setting free my astral body," Olof Jonsson has said.

> I have been able to give an account of happenings that were occurring at other locations at the same moment that my physical body sat under strict control.
>
> All these experiments in out-of-body projection have been carefully controlled, and my reports have been proved to agree with distant events. It has happened that a faint figure of my astral body, easily identifiable as me, has been caught on film.
>
> Sadly, the professor who took the picture died just a few years ago, and his wife, who had always detested his interest in parapsychology, burned all of his books, notes and effects. But some day, when the conditions are harmonious, I will do it again, *ja*.

Although that precious photograph no longer exists, a Swedish doctor testified that an image of Olof Jonsson once appeared in his home in Malmo:

> I met Olof Jonsson at a friend's party and immediately, and perhaps rudely, I expressed my skepticism. Although Jonsson had never been in my home, he went into what appeared to be a very light trance and described numerous particulars in my residence. When he described the children's bedroom, I began to lose my skepticism, but

when he went on to describe the children and give their names and ages, I became quite convinced of his abilities.

One night some weeks after Olof had visited my home to verify his impressions and to meet my family, I was disturbed from my reading in the front room by my daughter's delighted laughter. I hurried to her bedroom to inquire after her, since it was past her bedtime. When I asked her what had amused her so, she replied, "Oh, Father, that nice Mr. Jonsson was here smiling at us."

I telephoned Jonsson's apartment, but there was no answer. When I was at last able to contact him, I said, "I understand that you carried on an experiment with us tonight. My daughter saw you plainly in her bedroom where she and her brother sat reading."

Jonsson admitted that he had been sitting in a theater earlier that evening, waiting for a somewhat uninteresting film to run its course. Since his companion found the film fascinating, while Jonsson was bored, he decided to turn off his conscious mind and allow his astral self to wander. For some reason he found himself in our home, smiling at my daughter and son, who were both seated in their bedroom, reading.

Try a Sleep Projection

The preceding account is not related simply to chronicle another of Olof's many psychic feats, but to point out that we all, regardless of background, have certain abilities beyond those recognized in the conscious state of the physical world.

Try this. Just as you are falling off to sleep tonight, visualize yourself at a certain place. The time is now.

Observe all that is taking place, and look at every minute detail of your surroundings. What color is the carpeting--the draperies? What is on the table? Where is the davenport located? Is the door solid wood, or does it have a glass panel? Are there any strange odors--perfume, incense, garlic? Are there other people present? Do you know them? How are they dressed? What are they doing? Be observant.

This may not work the first few times you try it, but as soon as you "get back," make notes of everything you observed. Then if at all possible, check these things out for accuracy.

The place you visited, of course, should be a place you have never been before; but by the same token, it should be a place you know does exist, and where you can visit to check the details and impressions you have gained in the alpha state.

If you were wrong, do not be discouraged. Like anything else, conscious out-of-body projection takes practice, but in time you will probably find you are right more than wrong--and that's progress.

She Attended a Funeral in a Dream

The following account from *Fate* magazine for June 1968 gives us another remarkable story of a dreamer who projected to an actual scene that proved highly verifiable. Although the image of Jane Babrowicz was not seen by others, the images that she saw were true.

On a hot summer night in 1919, Jane Barrett (*nee* Babrowicz) was left alone in her house in Westford while her parents attended Aunt Lucy's funeral in Amsterdam, New York. A confident 12-year-old, Jane shunned her parents' offer to provide her with a baby-sitter.

As she lay in her bed trying to summon sleep on the torrid night, Jane hung suspended "in that limbo between wakefulness and sleep."

Then she seemed to feel herself rising toward the ceiling. Could she be dying?

She floated through the roof, out into the summer night, "propelled by some unknown force."

She saw a light in the distance toward which she seemed to be moving. When she reached it, she was surprised to find herself in a room that seemed somewhat familiar.

"Among the people in the room were my Uncle Harry, my grandmother, and others I did not know, all standing around quietly talking. Then I saw my own mother and father, and I knew where I was--at Aunt Lucy's funeral."

When her parents returned, Jane told them what she had seen. She described the arrangement of the casket, the color of Aunt Lucy's dress, and the style in which the deceased woman's hair had been fashioned.

"Not without some alarm, my parents confided that I was correct. Everything had been just as I described it. In a dream I had attended Aunt Lucy's funeral."

How Olof Jonsson Does It

In *The Psychic Feats of Olof Jonsson*, Brad reports a conversation with the famed mystic on how such a thing as out-of-body experience might be controlled.

Olof Jonsson: I can control such projection with my mind. First, I either lie on a couch or sit in a chair. Then I close my eyes and I concentrate on being outside of my body, looking at myself lying there. I *think* myself out of my body.

You actually will yourself out of the body?

Jonsson: Yes. I do this by concentrating on being outside of my body, looking at myself. After a couple of minutes, I can see myself lying there. Once I am free of my body, I think of all the different places I would like to visit--Malmo, Stockholm, Copenhagen--and then I wish me there. When I think of Malmo, the scenery just changes, and I am there. I can see the people around me, but they cannot see me. I can just walk around unencumbered.

Do you ever experience a rushing sensation or see multicolored lights?

Jonsson: No, nothing. I just feel completely harmonious...at one with the universe. I am in my *real* body, not my sluggish, physical shell.

When I am doing astral projection, it is a very happy time in my life. I do not miss the earthly life at all. The cares and considerations of the physical plane mean absolutely nothing to one who is in his astral body. The Earth dimension does not mean one thing to him.

Do you think that is what it will be like for you when you make the final projection, the final separation of mind from body?

Jonsson: Yes, I believe so. That final separation should be the happiest time in one's existence.

Olof Jonsson's method of achieving voluntary out-of-body projection:

> I lie down in a comfortable position, close my eyes, and relax until I reach the stage between waking and sleeping. Even though I am now into this hazy, in-between zone of consciousness, I still have full control over my mind.
>
> After a few moments, I begin to visualize myself outside of my body. Once one has become adept at astral projection, it takes no more than a matter of seconds until one's spiritual essence is floating above the physical body. When my Astral Self has been freed, I then visualize where I would like to be, and I am there instantly.
>
> It seems easier to visit family and friends when one is in the astral body. It appears quite evident that there exists some kind of force there to help draw one back.
>
> Hypnosis can be helpful in freeing the neophyte astral traveler from his body, but this method should be considered only if a good professional hypnotist of high repute and extensive experience in such matters is available.

Free of the Body!

"I have learned a great deal from my personal out-of-body experiences," Olof once reflected. "I have never used this ability to spy upon others or to attempt to learn things that others have decided to keep from me.

> No, what I have gained from astral projection is that calm and peace that can only come from being in harmony with the universe.
>
> I have learned to place the value of my fleshly body in its true perspective, and I have come to realize that the concerns and cares of the Earth plane are very insignificant indeed.

To be free of the flesh, to soar to other cities and countries completely unencumbered by time and space --what a happy thing!

Analyzing a Possible Out-of-Body Dream

Was the dream experience pleasurable or positive for you? ____

_____

Would you like to experience another such dream? _____

_____

Were you deliberately attempting to have such an experience, or was it spontaneous? _____

_____

If you deliberately sought to project your Essential Self during sleep, write down the most important steps in the technique that you used to accomplish a successful OBE. _____

_____
_____
_____
_____

If the dream was spontaneous, attempt a careful analysis of the circumstances that led to the experience. _____

_____
_____

1. What had you eaten for the evening meal (or the meal prior to the experience)? _____

_____

2. What was the basic nature of your thoughts immediately before falling asleep? _____

_____

_____

3. Have you been troubled or nervous about some approaching event, some potential crisis area, or about your rela-

tionship with someone? _____

_____

_____

Did you also experience any physical sensations at the time of the dream? Did you sense your spirit, your Essential Self, shifting to any particular part of your body? _____

_____

Did you notice any unusual physical circumstances when you returned to your body, such as heavy perspiration, extreme body temperature, sensations of hot or cold? _____

_____

Were you able to view your sleeping body as you left your physical form, or did you seem to rush away to another place? _____

_____

If you saw your body beneath you, take a moment to reflect upon your sensations as you viewed your sleeping physical form. __

_____

_____

Did you feel anything as your Essential Self moved through the walls or the ceiling? _____

If your answer to the previous question was yes, write down your memory of the sensation, the feeling, as carefully as you can. _____

_____

_____

Did you see anything beneath you as you traveled? Could you see clouds, fields, lakes, mountains, the lights of cities? _____

_____

If you were unable to perceive any aspects of the Earth-plane environment as you projected, what did you see as you traveled?

colors? _____

brilliant lights? _____

evidence of another dimension? _____

Were you aware of a guide that accompanied you through the experience? _____

Did you ever perceive any spirit forms near you or observing you? _____

Did you feel these entities were positive, negative, or some of each? _____

Was your destination a known place, a place in another dimension, an extraterrestrial environment, a place that still is unknown to you? _____
_____

Did you see anyone that you knew in this place? _____
_____

If you answered yes to the previous question, make a careful notation of that person's identity--relative, friend, acquaintance, etc. _____

If you traveled in a recognizable Earth-plane environment and if the people and the place of your destination were known to you, do you feel that they might have been aware of your presence?_____
_____

Is it possible that you materialized in corporeal form so that they might even have seen you? _____

Take several careful moments to analyze why your Essential Self directed itself to *that* location and to *those* people. Was the projection in answer to a need of yours, or could it have been in answer to a need of a person in the place of your destination? _____

_____

_____

If you traveled to a place in another dimension, did you recognize the entities or the essence of the entities with which you came in contact? _____

Did the entities communicate with you? _____

Write down the crux of the material that was relayed to you.

_____

_____

_____

_____

Was the communication meant to be shared with others or is the message for you alone? _____

What were your first thoughts immediately upon awakening from your OBE dream? _____

_____

_____

Did you tell anyone about the dream? _____

If so, who was the first person you told? _____

Write down a brief analysis of your true feelings about the OBE dream. _____

_____

_____

_____

_____

Achieving a Positive Dream Projection

The color-relaxation technique that we presented in Chapter 1 may be adapted into a most effective method of allowing you to experiment with a positive dream projection.

Find a time when you know that you will not be disturbed for at least an hour. You may wish to have a family member or a friend read the following technique in a soft, soothing voice while you sit or lie in a comfortable position. We also would suggest that gentle, restful music might be playing at a low volume in the background.

If you prefer, you may read the technique in your own voice and record the process on tape so that you might play the cassette back at your convenience and allow your own voice to guide you through the relaxation procedure. Some people feel that it is a very powerful experience to hear their own voice lulling them into a total state of relaxation and into the full receptivity that leads to productive dreaming.

Either method can be effective, and your success will depend upon your willingness to permit such a process to manifest in your unconscious.

Visualize that at your feet there lies a soft, warm blanket the color of rose. It has been learned that the color of rose stimulates natural body warmth and helps to induce sleep. It also provides one with a sense of well-being and a great feeling of being loved.

Imagine that you are mentally moving the rose-colored blanket to move slowly up over your body.

Feel it moving over your feet, relaxing them. Feel it moving over your legs, relaxing them. Feel it moving over your stomach, removing all tensions...over your back, removing all stress.

With every breath that you take, you find that you are becoming more and more relaxed. With every breath you take, you find that you are becoming more and more dreamy, reflective, peaceful.

Any sound that you might hear--a dog barking, a slamming door, a honking car horn--will not disturb you. Any sound that you hear will only help you to relax, to sleep, to dream.

Now feel that you are mentally pulling the rose-colored blanket over your chest, your arms, relaxing them, relaxing them.

As the blanket moves over your neck, relaxing all the muscles of your neck, visualize the rose-colored cloth transforming itself into a hood that covers your head like a cowl. Now you are enveloped completely in the beautiful, peaceful rose-colored blanket, and you feel the color of rose permeating your psyche, enabling you to fall into a deep sleep, a sleep that will allow dreams in which the Real You, your Essential Self, will soar free of your flesh form and move to Higher Dimensions of Reality.

The color green serves as a disinfectant and a cleanser. It also influences the proper receptivity of muscle and tissue to the healthful energy of deep sleep. Imagine that you are pulling a beautiful green blanket over your body.

Feel it moving over your feet, relaxing them, cleansing them, healing them.

Feel the lovely green blanket moving over your legs, healing them of all pains.

Feel it moving over your stomach, ridding it of all tensions.

Feel it moving over your chest, your arms, healing, relaxing, relaxing.

With every breath you take, feel yourself becoming more and more relaxed...more and more at peace, more and more at one with your mind and your body.

Feel the refreshing color of green moving over your back, relaxing all the stress along the spine. Feel the color of green cleansing, healing, relaxing your entire body.

As you make a hood of the green-colored blanket, pull it over your head, calming all of your nerves, your anxieties, your stresses. You are now completely enveloped in the healing color of green, and you feel it permeate your psyche, relaxing you, calming you, allowing you to have marvelous dreams of soaring free of Time and Space, free of all limitations, free of all physical boundaries.

The color of gold has long been recognized as a great strengthener of the nervous system. It also aids digestion, helps you to become calm, and allows you to have a deep and restful sleep.

Visualize now that you are pulling a soft, beautiful gold blanket slowly over your body.

Feel it moving over your feet, calming you. Feel it moving over your legs, relaxing them. Feel it moving over your stomach, soothing any nervous condition, healing any stomach upset.

Feel the lovely, relaxing gold blanket moving over your chest, your arms, your back.

Nothing will disturb you, nothing will distress you. All stressful thoughts are leaving you. All concerns are being left behind as you become more and more relaxed...more and more relaxed...more and more prepared to have beautiful, golden dreams.

Feel the gold blanket fashioning itself into a protective hood that covers your head and completely bathes you in the color of gold. Feel the color of gold permeating your brain, your mind, your nervous system, permitting your body-mind network to create a healthier and happier you. Relax...relax...as you prepare to travel in your Spirit Body to receive wonderful, golden teaching dreams from a Higher Intelligence.

Now visualize at your feet a blanket the color of blue. The color blue prompts psychic sensitivity and provides one with a sense of accomplishment and confidence. The color of blue will aid you greatly in being able to soar through Time and Space free of your physical body and to experience an out-of-body projection of a positive and helpful nature.

Imagine that you are now willing the blue-colored blanket to move slowly up your body. Feel it moving over your feet, relaxing them. Feel it moving over your legs, your hips, relaxing them.

With every breath you take, you are becoming more and more relaxed...more and more ready to fall into a deep, deep sleep, more and more ready to dream wonderful, beautiful dreams of soaring through Time and Space, of moving through the clouds, of contacting the stars, of touching the very heart of the Universe. With every breath you take, you are more and more at peace. . .at one with the universe.

Now you feel the blue blanket moving over your chest, your arms, your back. You feel it moving over your stomach, removing all tensions; over your back, removing all stresses.

Everywhere the blue blanket touches you, you feel a wonderful, relaxing energy moving throughout every cell of your body. Everywhere the blue blanket touches you, you feel relaxed... relaxed...relaxed.

Now as the blue blanket becomes a beautiful blue cowl, imagine that the color of blue is about to permeate your psyche and give you the wisdom to accomplish all of life's important tasks in a positive way. Know that the color of blue will do its part in activating your dream machinery to produce dreams of meaningful out-of-body projections. Feel the color of blue accelerating all of your psychic abilities.

Now bring the beautiful blue cowl over your head and let it completely envelope you in its peaceful, relaxing, loving energy.

You now have the ability to leave the fleshly shell of your physical body and soar free of Time and Space. You know that you are surrounded by Love and protected by benevolent energy from the very heart of the Universe. You know that you have the ability to soar free of Time and Space and to travel without fear anywhere that you wish.

Feel your Essential Self, your Spirit Body, leaving its fleshly domicile. Feel your Essence moving free of its clothing of bone and flesh. Feel the Real You projecting from the body shell and soaring into Higher Dimensions.

At the count of five you will be wherever it is that you wish to be--at the side of a loved one who is separated from you by physical time and space, at the scene of a place that you have always wished to visit, at the side of someone you admire. You know that at the count of five you will have the ability to be wherever it is that you wish to be. **One**: feel your Essence projecting through limitless Time and Space. **Two**: feel yourself moving toward your desired goal. **Three**: the person or place is becoming clearer in your view. **Four**: sharper and sharper, clearer and clearer as you move closer and closer. **Five**: you are there! Feel that you are there. See that you are there. Know that you are there!

(Permit about ten seconds to pass before repeating the instructions: "Feel that you are there. See that you are there. Know that you are there!" Now allow a minute to pass.)

At the count of three, you will take special notice of any unusual details present in your target area. See and remember any special circumstances. Notice if there is anything different or unusual about the person that you wished to visit. You have the ability to remember anything important that will later prove to you that you were actually here in this place, here with this person, in your Spirit Body.

(Allow about one minute for this examination of the target person and place.)

Now you are moving back to your flesh form, back to your

physical body. You are returning to your earthly shell; you are moving effortlessly through Time and Space to return safely to the physical form in which your Soul presently resides.

At the count of five, you will be safely back in your physical body, filled with all that you need to remember for your good and your gaining, feeling better than you have felt in weeks and weeks, months and months. **One**: coming back to the body. **Two**: feeling better than you have felt in weeks and weeks. **Three**: coming back feeling very, very good in mind, body, and spirit. **Four**: coming back to the body filled with love. **Five**: back in the body and feeling great!

Chapter 8

Dreams of UFO Contact

Each of the authors has had an experience with an extraterrestrial or multidimensional being that has convinced him/her that we are not alone in the Universe.

Dreams of UFO contact experiences may provide you with a fascinating mechanism for receiving teachings from a higher intelligence or from a higher aspect of your own marvelous Self. Physical contact with The Other may actually be a kind of illumination experience that has cloaked itself in trappings of a most colorful kind.

It is not advisable to set about to make a deliberate contact with "UFO intelligences," for to do so may bring about certain psychological dangers. It just does not seem mentally healthful to meditate, concentrate, and focus one's energy upon reaching entities that may be from other worlds or other dimensions.

We feel that true contact comes from a kind of process of selection that we never may be able to fathom totally. By the same token we feel that you can make yourself receptive to receive dream teachings and to program your dream scenario to dress themselves in costumes of extraterrestrial encounters.

The Universe and Your Imagination

As John Wheeler of Princeton University has stated

In some strange sense this is a participatory universe. What we have been accustomed to call physical reality turns out to be largely a papier-mâché construction of our imagination plastered in between the solid iron pillars of our observations. These observations constitute the only reality. Until we see why the universe is built this way, we have not understood the first thing about it.... We will first understand how simple the universe is when we recognize how strange it is.

We think the same thing may be true of the entire UFO mystery. It may one day be revealed to all of us as a remarkably simple construct, when once we realize how wonderfully strange it is. That involves our participation and our interaction as integral elements of a greater reality. Basically, we have come to the conclusion that some external intelligence has interacted with humankind throughout history in an effort to learn more about us or in an effort to communicate certain basic truths and concepts to our species.

A Symbiotic Relationship Between Them and Us

We also are convinced that there is a subtle kind of symbiotic relationship that exists between humankind and those beings that we label UFO intelligences.

In some way that we have yet to determine, they need us as much as we need them. It is quite possible that either one or both of our species may once have had an extraterrestrial origin, but the important thing is that the very biological and spiritual evolution of Earth may depend upon the establishment of equilibrium between us and our cosmic cousins.

UFOs may be our neighbors right around the corner in another Space-Time continuum. It may even be, in some cases, that what we have been labeling spaceships may actually be multidimensional mechanisms or psychic constructs of these paraphysical beings.

Whoever these intelligences are, they appear to have the ability to influence the human mind telepathically in order to project what may appear to be three-dimensional images to the witnesses of UFO activity.

The image seen may depend in large part upon the preconceptions that the witness has about alien life-forms, and this accounts for reported accounts of UFO occupants running the gamut from bug-eyed-monster types to little gray men to metaphysical space brothers.

Space Brothers

The space brother concept is very popular and is becoming more so with the work of people who, for whatever reasons, like to see the UFO in terms of deliverance. There seems to be a great need right now for cosmic messiahs when it appears as though nuclear war is upon us, when we must face the grim specter of our having raped and plundered the Earth Mother, when we must recognize the extent to which the ecological systems might give away. There seems to be a great need to believe or to hope that some ET saviors are going to come out of the sky in the UFO and take us away to a beautiful new planet.

This seems to go back to the old beliefs in certain aspects of Christianity that the "Elect" will be saved and taken away on the clouds by the returning energy of Jesus.

We believe that Christ Consciousness always is available to us on the Earth plane, and at this particular time in a kind of cosmic cycle, it may be becoming more available to those who want to embark upon a life of meditation, of Self-discipline, and of reaching out to touch and become a part of the Christ Consciousness.

Look to the Stars

The idea of being taken away to another planet appears to be a hope born of desperation for many people.

It is understandable that humankind always looks for deliverance. As it says in the Bible, "Look unto the hills," or look upward, "from whence cometh thy help."

There seems to be a reflex action to look to the stars from whence we know our inner being came. We are the stuff of the stars, and this great nostalgia to return has become transformed into a desperation to escape. We have to balance that longing, and the various "space brothers" appear to be entities that materialize in the form of biblical or idealistic angel-type entities to tell us that we must clean up our planet and our entire human "act."

The basic message of the space brothers always has been that we must learn to control our bad manners and our nuclear bombardments, and that we must do something about getting the planet together in harmony.

The Symbology of the UFO

One thing about the UFO entities is that the mechanism employed by them always is relevant to the witnesses' time context. That is, in earlier times they appeared and declared themselves to be elves or angels. Now they declare themselves very often to be UFOnauts, men or women from other planets.

The form in which the UFO construct appears, and the symbology it employs, are always timeless and instantly recognizable at one level of the beholder's consciousness. Elves, fairies, and angelic beings, it would seem, have been popular in all cultures and in all recorded time. The complete experience of any witness to UFO activity is quite probably a part of a natural process, whose *actual purpose* is staggeringly complex for desperately throbbing human minds and brains to deal with in this moment in time and space.

It may be that the UFO mystery is primarily subjective and symbolic. There are, of course, objective aspects, too, but the basic mechanics seem to deal on the level of the unconscious mind. Perhaps the entire phenomenon is a way of programming the human mind to accept a greater and more meaningful physical contact of true *physical* beings in our very near future.

One can argue on and on whether the UFO entities are in reality nonphysical entities from an invisible realm in our own world, or if they are physical beings who have the ability to create a state of invisibility so that they may materialize and dematerialize both their bodies and their vehicles before the eyes of startled witnesses. Or if they truly are UFOnauts who come from another physical world for the purpose of investigating our planet preparatory to some mass landing or some important communication and revelation.

Perhaps all these theories are correct. We may be confronted by several kinds of intelligences in our spiritual, intellectual, biological, evolutionary process. Or we may be dealing with an intelligence that has a physical structure so totally unlike ours that it presents itself in a variety of disguises and at times employs invisibility, materialization, and dematerialization in order to accomplish its goal of communication with us.

Intelligences From Higher Dimensions

Through the UFO contactees the space brothers speak often of an impending New Age, wherein humankind will obtain a new consciousness, a new awareness in a higher state--or frequency--of vibration. They speak of each physical body being in a state of vibration and of all things vibrating at individual frequencies.

Those who claim to speak to the space brothers say that the UFO intelligences come from higher dimensions all around our own, but they function on different vibratory levels, just as there are various radio frequencies operating simultaneously in our environment.

We can attune ourselves to these higher dimensions through much the same manner as a radio receiver tunes into the frequencies of broadcasting stations. The UFO entities therefore travel on different frequencies, according to their vibratory rate.

In *Mysteries of Time and Space* Brad suggested that some undeclared paraphysical opponents have engaged our species in what he has come to call the reality game. When we have apprehended the true significance of this contest, we will obtain such control of our life and our abilities that we will confront all aspects of existence with the same ease and freedom with which we would enter a game.

We believe that this is a glorious way to approach life, truly reflective of our noble star-seeded heritage.

Wisdom from the Firestar

In the mid-1960s, when she was a seminarian and later a staff member at the Lutheran School of Theology in Chicago, Sherry began to read the scriptures with a new vision. She had come to perceive that the creation story and the account of beings from the spirit world taking human wives contained certain elements that sounded very much like beings from the "powers and principalities" mentioned so often in the Bible.

In 1974, although it was foreign to her conservative reserve, she found herself in the presence of a psychic-sensitive who told her that she was a "stranger to Earth" and that she had come from "beyond our solar system" with "outer space attunements with religion, metaphysics, and an understanding of the Divine."

The psychic spoke for over an hour--until she fainted. The reading left Sherry puzzled with such statements as ""...your body is being altered;" Certain cells within your brain are awakening;" and "Telepathic contacts are being beamed to you from outer space."

In 1983 Sherry came out of a deep meditation to hear a very melodic female voice saying, "Sister, do not be frightened. I am Semjase."

Sherry was only dimly aware that certain UFO contactees identified Semjase (Sem-YA-see) as a cosmonaut from the Pleiades.

As she listened attentively, the entity told her that within three days a Dr. Fred Bell would call her and that she was to pay close attention to what he would say.

Amazingly, Dr. Bell did telephone Sherry within three days. He informed her that he had been in contact with the Pleiadean and that Semjase had contacted him for the first time in three years with the message that he must take Sherry Hansen to the "Firestar."

It was impossible to dismiss such an eerie prophetic message, and arrangements were made for Sherry to undergo a meditative process that had been given to Dr. Bell by Semjase. Incredibly, a Light Being took Sherry out of her body for five hours.

"I was guided through the most mystically beautiful experience of my life," Sherry has remarked.

> It seems as though the Light Being and I traveled through galaxies, making stops along the way. There was one place, perhaps it was the New Jerusalem, that was like a crystal or a diamond planet, reflecting and refracting

the most beautiful colors, lovely beyond compare. As a living crystal, I became fused with the light...I became the light.

The Living Myth of the UFO

Distinguished scholar Joseph Campbell has observed that the most important function of a living mythological symbol is to waken and to give guidance to the energies of life.

The living mythological symbol not only "turns a person on," but it also turns him in a specific direction that enables him to participate effectively in a functioning social group.

Dr. John W. Perry has identified the living mythological symbol as "an effect image," an image that speaks directly to the feeling system and instantly elicits a response.

If this symbol must first be read by the brain, it is already a dead symbol and will not produce responding resonance within the witness. When the vital symbols of any given social group are able to evoke such resonances within all its members "...a sort of magical cord unites them as one spiral organism, functioning through members, who, though separate in space, are one in being and belief."

In *Gods of Aquarius*, Brad puts forth his contention that the UFO phenomenon provides contemporary humanity with a vital living mythological symbol, an effect image that communicates to our Essential Selves, bypassing our brains, evading acculturation, manipulating historical conditioning.

The UFO as Transformative Symbol

We believe that the UFO may be here to serve humankind as a transformative symbol that will unite our entire species as one spiritual organism, functioning through members who, though separate in space, are yet one in being and belief.

To suggest that the UFO is a living mythological symbol does not diminish its reality in an objective, physical sense. The UFO may ultimately be more real than the transitory realities of computers, machines, associations, political parties, or political detentes. It may well be that it will be through the cosmic catharsis of dreams, visions, and inspirations that the UFO phenomenon will come to be the spiritual midwife who will bring about our true star-birth into the Universe.

Analyzing Your "Outer Space Connection"

In *The Fellowship* we set forth the thesis that throughout history some kind of external intelligence has interacted with humankind. Indeed, there appears to be some kind of symbiotic relationship that exists between us and the UFO intelligences, regardless of whether they be extraterrestrial or multidimensional entities.

Contactees, those people who claim to have established communication with UFO beings, may be the emerging prototypes of a "new evangelism," a blending of science and traditional religious truths. It would seem that we are on the edge of a quantum leap forward on both our biological and spiritual levels of being, if we may believe the contactees and their otherworldly correspondents.

UFO abductees, those men and women who claim that they have been "kidnapped" aboard spacecraft, appear upon first examination to present a more sinister aspect of the contact experience. Closer analyses--such as those we present in *The UFO Abductors*--must be brought to bear upon this piece of the Great Cosmic Jigsaw Puzzle before any meaningful assessment might be made. It may be that there is a cosmic war being waged, and Earth may be a battleground for the forces of Light and Darkness.

If you have experienced vivid dreams of UFOs and extra-terrestrial or multidimensional entities, you may be having contact with other intelligences while you sleep. On the other hand, you may be experiencing something more than dreams.

Answer the following questions with honesty and some degree of reflection.

Have you ever had dreams that contain any of the following scenarios?

_____Viewing a city or a planet made of crystal or diamonds

_____Being in a doctor's examination room with smallish figures (or other entities) examining you

_____Receiving teachings in an unusual classroom
_____Being able to fly, like Superman
_____Viewing the Earth from a perspective away from the planet
_____Eating a strange food that is offered to you
_____Drinking a peculiar liquid that is offered to you
_____Seeing Earth as it might have appeared in prehistoric times
_____Perceiving yourself as the member of a UFO crew
_____Observing yourself coming to Earth as a Being of Light
_____Sensing yourself encircled by smallish entities
_____Having the sensation of being drawn aboard a UFO to receive instructions
_____Watching yourself in "biblical" times or communicating with religious figures

Our research has indicated that a great number of those people who have undergone UFO experiences have had many of the following "problems." When Sherry was UFO expert Dr. J. Allen Hynek's manager, she noticed that he also had accumulated data that showed similarities in physical anomalies among the contactees and abductees. How many of the difficulties below have at some time in your life troubled you?
_____sinusitis
_____scars from unknown causes
_____unexplained soreness of the eyes
_____unusual skin rashes
_____an unexplained hole in the eardrum
_____an unexplained puncture mark in the navel
_____painful and swollen joints
_____pain in the back of the neck
_____adrenal problems

From the thousands of contactees who have filled out our questionnaires, a remarkable pattern has begun to emerge. Do you have any of the following?
_____extra or transitional vertebrae
_____very sharp eyesight
_____keen hearing
_____strong sense of smell

_____low blood pressure
_____Rh negative blood
_____hypersensitivity to electricity
_____a "normal" body temperature lower than 98.6
_____an adverse reaction to high humidity
_____an unusual blood type
_____hypersensitivity to light
_____difficulty in dealing with emotions
_____a persistent inner feeling of great urgency

Have you experienced any of the following?
_____a head injury that knocked you unconscious
_____a near-death experience
_____a life-threatening illness
_____hypnosis
_____deep meditative states
_____mind-altering drugs
_____a psychological "peak" experience
_____an illumination experience
_____an intense religious experience
_____a severe accident
_____a divorce (yours or your parents)
_____a "missing time" experience

During the course of your life experiences, have you ever encountered any of the following?
_____an invisible playmate
_____the visitation of an angel
_____the sighting of an elf
_____a nature spirit
_____a fairy
_____the manifestation of a Light Being
_____the appearance of a holy figure
_____Bigfoot
_____a ghost
_____a spirit guide
_____the spirit of a departed loved one
_____a glowing ball of light

_____alien entities
_____bedroom apparitions that seemed real

Which of the following have you perceived?
_____telepathy
_____prior life memories
_____out-of-body experience
_____auras
_____white light in meditation
_____a oneness with the Universe
_____healings
_____automatic writing
_____communication/channeling from higher intelligence
_____clairvoyance
_____prophecy
_____spirit entities

Were you interested in UFOs before your dream or your personal contact experience? _____

Have any members of your family or your friends had UFO dreams or contact experiences? _____

If you believe that you have experienced a UFO encounter, was the contact physical (that is, did you actually go on board a craft or communicate with entities who were solidly three-dimensional) or was the encounter a mental/spiritual one, taking place in a dream, a vision, or an out-of-body experience? _____
_____
_____

If you believe that you have experienced "missing time," have you since received any memory flashes of what occurred on board the craft or in the presence of the entities? _____
_____

If you believe that you may have been an abductee, do you feel that you were enlisted in the experience against your will?

Do you evaluate your UFO dreams or encounters as basically positive or negative experiences? _____

Do you feel that the experience was in any way comparable to an illumination or cosmic-consciousness type of experience? _____

If you believe that you received a kind of contact or communication from UFO entities in your dream or in an actual physical encounter, do you feel that you have received any messages that should be shared with others? If your answer is yes, summarize that message. _____

_____

_____

Do you believe that you may have lived a prior existence on another planet or in another dimension? _____

State briefly your basic views toward the UFO phenomenon. Why are they here? From where do they originate? Are they "good" or "evil"? _____

_____

_____

_____

Contacting a UFOnaut in Your Dreams

The following creative visualization is one that should work very well in creating the proper attitude for a dream of UFO contact. It may enable you actually to simulate the contact experience. You may be able to obtain certain benefits and knowledge from the experience that will satisfy your desire to make an actual contact with UFO beings. The most important thing to remember is to work diligently on developing yourself spiritually, then if actual UFO contact is to occur to you, it will happen at the proper time.

An added advantage may be that, while preparing yourself

in such a positive way, you actually will summon a facet of Higher Awareness to you while you are in the altered state of consciousness. You may use any of the inductions that have been provided to you in previous chapters. As before, you may engage the assistance of a trusted individual to read the induction and the suggestions to you, or you may record the instructions in your own voice prior to the experience.

We recommend that you play some very restful, relaxing music to aid you in drifting into an altered state of consciousness. The music should not be a popular melody with a refrain, nor should it contain vocalizations. Instrumental with nonassociative emotional response will be best. You may even use the soundtrack to such motion pictures as *Close Encounters of the Third Kind*, or *E.T.* We strongly recommend some of the New Age music of Steven Halpern, Michael Stern, or Iasos.

You either may be sitting or lying down, whichever position is the most comfortable for you. Be certain that your legs and arms remain uncrossed, however, so that you do not shut off normal circulation during the experience.

Relax yourself completely and let every muscle relax. Let your mind begin to drift and float, then undergo as complete an induction as possible, going as deep within an altered state of consciousness as you are able to achieve.

After the induction has been repeated, and a state of relaxation has been achieved, the following should be said:

You have permitted your body to fall asleep, but your mind has remained aware. You have permitted your body to fall asleep, so that your mind, the Real You, can make contact with a being that you call an extraterrestrial, or a multidimensional, entity.

Your mind is now beginning to soar to the in-between Universe between this Universe, between this world of physical reality, and the world of the Eternal Now. Your mind is beginning to soar to the place where it can best make contact with a higher intelligence.

As your body lies in a deep sleep, your mind, your Essential Self, is aware of a large globe. A large golden globe is moving toward you. You see it coming down like a giant Christmas tree ornament. A golden round ornament is moving toward you.

Now you see that the ornament is beginning to fade away. As it touches the ground next to you, it fades away. Standing before you is an intelligence that you know has come from another world. This may be an actual physical world or it may be a multidimensional plane of existence. Whichever it is, you know that this entity means you no harm. This entity has come in peace.

This entity has come to express unconditional love toward you, and you feel a great sense of being loved unconditionally by this intelligence. You are encouraged to walk forward to extend your hand and to grasp the hand of this multidimensional/extraterrestrial being.

Become totally aware of this entity. See the clothes that it is wearing.

Do your best to identify the sex of this being. Is it male or female? Is it one sex or the other? Is it androgynous? Does it seem, rather, to be a subtle mixture of the sexes?

See his body, his face. Take careful notice of his eyes, his mouth. Look at the hands. Are the hands the same as yours?

How tall is the being? What color is the being's skin? What type of skin does the being have? Is it rough? Is it furred? Is it feathered? Is it smooth? Does it appear much like your own?

Notice all that you can of the being, and become totally aware of this multidimensional or extraterrestrial being.

Now the being telepathically is sending you images of his world. You are now seeing a city as it is in his planet or his multidimensional world.

Through the magic of this telepathy, you are visualizing yourself walking through the streets of an alien city with your new friend. Become fully aware of the environment. What do you most notice about this city and this other physical or mental world?

Are there other entities such as the one walking at your side moving about on the streets?

What do you observe about the methods of transportation?

What type of buildings do the entities live in? Are they transparent or translucent?

In what type of activity do the beings seem to be most engaged?

Are you walking on a sidewalk, or are you somehow being levitated? Are you being carried in some way as you move through the city in this other world?

Now you understand that you are approaching the home in which this entity lives. You have been invited to enter the private dwelling place of this entity from another world. Take a moment now to experience fully your emotions as you walk or move toward the home.

Understand the expectations that you are feeling at this time.

Are there plants that grow near this home?

Are there animals moving near? Look at the animals. Be aware if there are any creatures that you would understand as birds or insects.

Now you are entering your alien friend's home. Be aware of your inner thoughts and feelings.

Notice *how* you enter the being's home. Is there a portal or a door that opens, or do you simply find yourself within the structure?

The being gestures to you that you should be seated, and he hands you an object that you understand to be a drink container. It is filled with liquid that you are to drink. You understand telepathically that it is your host's favorite drink.

Put it to your lips and savor it gratefully. Taste the drink in your mouth. Be very aware of the taste. Be aware of any sensations that you have as the liquid moves down your throat.

Now the being is handing you a plate. On the plate, you understand, is the being's favorite food.

Look at the utensil that he hands you. How closely does it resemble a fork or a spoon?

Place the food upon the utensil, and place the food in your mouth. Savor the food, taste it, and be aware of the texture. Chew the food if necessary; swallow it. Be aware of any sensations or emotions that you may experience as you swallow the food.

Now you are being shown something that you understand relates to a television set. It is a communicating device. What to you see on the device? What do you hear coming from it? What unique sights or sounds impress themselves upon your senses?

The being points with pride at what you understand appropriately to be a library. How does the library represent itself?

The being now indicates to you that he will permit you to ask any questions that you wish to know about him or his world. He listens carefully, and he indicates to you that he will very thoughtfully answer your questions and answer them truthfully.

You will receive the answers telepathically. You will receive full understanding of his answers. You may ask any question you wish about their technology, religion, government, or the cultural structure of their world; he will answer you truthfully. Ask your first question now. (*Pause for 60 seconds.*)

What kind of reply did he give you? What answer did you receive?

Be certain that you understood completely what he told you. What do you feel about what you have learned?

Are you pleased or displeased with the answer?

How do you feel now about this entity from another world? Do you feel positive or negative?

The ET or multidimensional being is indicating that you may ask another question if you so desire. If you wish, ask him another question. Once again you will receive the answer telepathically. Be certain that you completely understand what he tells you.

Ask the question now. (*Pause for 60 seconds.*)

Now the entity is telling you that he must return you to your world, to your dimension, and as he is saying good-bye to you, he reaches in a drawer in the wall and brings forth an object. He tells you that it is a very special gift that he wishes to present to you. He wishes you to take the gift with you.

Look at it. See what it is. Tell the entity how you feel about him, about his gift. Say good-bye, for now you must leave.

As you feel yourself moving through space, back to the present moment, back to the world of reality in which you must live, you focus your thoughts on the entity from the other physical or nonphysical world. You remember his answers to your questions, and you pay special attention to the gift that he presented to you.

Open your hands and look at the gift once again. Turn it over in your hands. Smell it. Feel it. Discover all that you can about the gift.

Did you notice anything about the gift when he gave it to you?

What deep significance will this gift have for you?

Know that you have the ability to use the gift wisely and to its most positive advantage.

When you return to full consciousness, you will hold the images of this vision in your mind for as long as you can.

It is important that you hold the thought forms as long as possible so that you can impress that energy upon material-plane substance. The images of life substance will open your desire so completely that they will soon condense into patterns that will help prepare you for future contact with extraterrestrials or multi-dimensional beings.

At the count of five, you will be fully awake. **One**: coming awake. **Two**: coming more and more awake. **Three**: feeling very, very good and coming awake. **Four**: coming awake, feeling very good. **Five**: waking up with a big smile, feeling very good and very positive.

Making Dream Contact with a UFO

After a deep induction, have the following read to you by a trusted friend or by your own voice previously recorded.

You are visualizing yourself standing or sitting on a peaceful beach, a lonely country road, a mountain pass (whichever you prefer). You look up at the night sky, splashed with brilliant stars. You can see the sky from horizon to horizon. You feel in harmony with the Earth and sky.

As you are looking up at the stars, you begin to notice a particularly brilliant, flashing star high over head. As you watch it, it seems to be moving toward you. It seems to be lowering itself to you.

Now you see it is not a star at all. It is a beautifully glowing object. You feel no fear, only expectation. You feel secure in the love of the Universe.

You know that your guide is near to you and no negative entity can make contact with you. You feel unconditional love as the object with the sparkling, swirling light lowers itself near you. You know it is a vehicle that has come to take you to levels of higher awareness.

A door opens in the side of the lighted vehicle. You look inside and see that it is glowing with a beautiful, purple-colored light. You know that it is safe. It glows within with the purple light of the highest vibration. Beyond that is a golden light that you know provides protection. You know that this golden light is of unconditional love from the very heart of the Universe.

You see someone coming to meet you from the very heart of the Universe.

You see someone coming to meet you from the vehicle's interior. You see entities that you know have come from another world.

Look at the size of the entities. Notice how they are dressed.

Take careful notice of the shape of their bodies, eyes, and mouths.

See the way they move, the way they walk.

See the way they hold their hands. Understand that they mean you no harm.

Let them take you by the hand. Let them lead you within the light vehicle that is hovering above the Earth.

You feel love, pure unconditional love all around you. You know that you are safe. You know that these beings are benevolent. You know that they have come from another planet; perhaps another Universe.

Step inside the vehicle. Become totally aware of the objects, the technology, the communication devices. Be aware of all that you see inside, and know that you will be able to remember.

As you move into the light vehicle--the spaceship that has moved through space and time to make contact with you, to make contact with planet Earth--you are aware of one entity that stands before you as the leader. Become totally aware of this leader from another planet.

See his particular clothing. The shape of his body, his face, his eyes, his mouth. The way he holds his hands. The way he moves his body.

He indicates that you should be seated before him. You are being shown communication devices on the walls around you that indicate this object's origin. You are understanding these things in terms that you can understand. You know from what planet, from what galaxy, these beings have come.

They are open, friendly. They have nothing but love for you.

They are keeping nothing from you. They will answer any questions that you wish to ask.

Experience your emotions as you sit before the leader of this extraterrestrial expedition to Earth. See the type of illumination that issues from the walls. Be aware of any aromas, any sounds, any signs of unusual movement or activity.

There are unique statues and paintings arranged around the spacecraft. These are statues and paintings that represent life on a faraway planet. Look at them. Remember them.

The leader now is showing you what appears to be a great transparent cube that is supported on a metallic tripod. As you lean forward to stare into the cube, the leader of the extraterrestrial expedition tells you that you now will be permitted to see a meaningful vision of life on his planet.

He tells you that you will see all that you need to see at this moment for your good and your gaining. You will see all that is necessary for your present level of understanding.

You will see a vision of his world that will be completely individualized for you, in your particular needs in your world.

See that vision now. (*Pause for 60 seconds.*)

Now you will be able to ask any question of the leader--you may wish to know something that will help you better understand extraterrestrial life, how you might make effective contact with extraterrestrials, how you might better communicate with higher forms of intelligence. Ask that question now. (*Pause for 60 seconds.*)

Now the leader is telling you that it is time for you to return to your world. It is time to go back to the human reality. It is time to leave the light vehicle. It is time to leave the spaceship that came from another world.

You will remember all that you need to know for your good and your gaining. Because of your experience with the extraterrestrials, you will be strengthened to face the challenges and the learning experiences of your life on Earth.

Know this: The more you share your visions and the teachings that you received from the ETs, the more your understanding of them will grow.

You are now awakening, surrounded by light and by pure unconditional love. You will feel very good in mind and spirit.

You will feel better than you have felt in weeks, in months and months, in years. You will awaken fully at the count of five.

Chapter 9

Dream Teachings from the Future

Is it possible to dream the future? Is it possible to move through Time to view scenes from the future and from other probable realities?

These questions are as old as humankind, but for the spiritual seeker they take on several different gradations of meaning. The initial secret of dreaming the future may be found in recognizing and accepting one of the basic tenets of Amerindian medicine power: Time is nonlinear, it moves in a spiral, a cycle, rather than a straight line.

Oh, yes, of course Time moves in a linear course in the material, Earth-plane reality construct; but we are speaking now of the Greater Reality. We are speaking of the dimensions that truly shape the profound perimeters of what is real and what is nonreal.

Can we, then, foresee the course of future events in our dreams, or is everything inexorably preordained?

It is perhaps not so much a question of humanity's free will as it is a matter of what truly constitutes Time.

"In any attempt to bridge the domains of experience belonging to the spiritual and physical sides of our nature," wrote A.S. Eddington, "Time occupies the key position."

From the spiritual perspective, the concept of Time entertained by the technologists and the general masses of humankind is a naive one. The overwhelming number of physical thinkers around us see Time as an absolute, because that is the pattern in which humankind's sensory apparatus has evolved throughout the several centuries of our cerebral existence.

Dream Future Possibilities

The vast testimony of "precognitive" dreams that foresee the future have convinced many serious thinkers that certain men and women have occasionally broken loose from the evolved sensory pattern to receive a glimpse of the true order of the Universe. Dreams are immediate evidence that humanity is nonphysical as well as physical. Dreams are paranormal phenomena with which everyone can identify. Only the most cynical (and, we should add, inexperienced or insensitive) deny the richness or the value of the dream experience.

Precognitive dreams may show us future possibilities or future actualities. They may indicate what *may happen* if we pursue a certain course of action, and they may show us a *precise event* which, seemingly, cannot be altered.

"Knowing" You Have Seen Tomorrow

There is a "knowing" that suffuses your entire being when you have viewed a future actuality dream or vision. The "noetic" quality of precognition is known to many of you, we are certain. Many of you have had "hunches" that you knew were totally correct--regardless of how many people told you you were mistaken. You have all had those times when you knew that you were right in doing what you had to do.

What occurs when one has truly glimpsed the future?

We have had precognitive dreams and visions of both profound and exceedingly mundane occurrences. So have you. When you had such an experience, could you have changed that future event?

In our opinion a foreknowledge of the future resides at some level of the subconscious. The level that is aware occasionally flashes a dramatic bit or a scene to the conscious mind in a dream or in meditation. The foreknowledge of the future also is founded on the knowledge of how the individual will use his freedom of choice.

In other words, the "future event" thus conditions the subconscious Self. The level of the subconscious that "knows" the future does not condition the "future event." The transcendent element of the Self that knows what "will be" blends all Time into "what is now and what always will be."

For the conscious Self, what is now the past was once the future.

The fact that a level of the psyche may know the future does not mean that the conscious Self has no freedom of choice. Simply stated, if the future could be changed, it would not be the future. In a true precognitive experience when one perceives the future, he or she has glimpsed what will be and what, for a certain level of the subconscious, already exists.

The Five Types of Precognitive Experiences

There are, perhaps, five types of precognitive experiences. At the most elementary level is a *subliminal precognition* or the "hunch" that proves to be an accurate one. There is absolutely no slur intended in labeling this type of experience as "elementary." Some hunches have saved lives and established many giants of industry and commerce.

Next would come *trivial precognition*, which takes only a short time before the actual occurrence of a rather unimportant event.

Then, in the areas of full-blown, meaningful precognitions--which indicate a power of mind not limited by Time or Space--there are *beneficial*, *nonbeneficial*, and *detrimental previsions*.

In a beneficial premonition the transcendent level of Self may overdramatize a future event in such a way that it proves to be a warning that is acted upon by the conscious Self's characteristic reaction to a crisis.

An Experiment with Time

In *An Experiment with Time*, J. W. Dunne provides many examples of his own precognitive dreams, which he recorded over a period of several years. He firmly believed in sleep and in dreams as the prime openers of the subconscious, and he formulated a philosophy called "Serialism" to account for precognition.

In Dunne's view, Time was an "Eternal Now." All events that have ever occurred, that exist now, or that ever will be, are everlastingly in existence. In our ordinary, conscious, waking state, he writes, our view is only of the present. In sleep, however, our view might be sufficiently enlarged to allow several glimpses of the future.

The philosophy of Serialism offers the challenge of bold and imaginative thinking. For example, his thought in regard to déja vu, the sense of the already seen, is quite intriguing. Dunne suggests that this curious experience (that nearly everyone has had at one time or another) of "having been here before" is due to the stimulation of a partially remembered precognitive dream. When the conversation becomes familiar or the new location becomes suddenly recognizable, one may, according to Dunne, simply be remembering a precognitive dream that had been driven back into the subconscious.

The Future Dimension

We have always loved Saint Augustine's bemused evaluation of the nature of Time. "Time?" he puzzled. "What is it? If nobody asks me, I know. But if I am asked, I do not know!"

For the spiritual seeker it soon becomes obvious that the conventional idea of Time existing as some sort of stream flowing along in one dimension is an inadequate one. In this view the past does not exist; it is gone forever. The future does not exist because it has not yet happened. The only thing that exists is the present moment.

But the present does not really exist, either; for it is no sooner "now" than that "now" becomes part of the past. What was the future when you began to read this chapter was fleetingly the present and already has become the past by the time you will read the next word.

If the past completely ceased to exist, we should have no memory of it. Yet each of us has a large and varied memory bank. Therefore, we know that the past must exist in *some* sense; not, perhaps, as a physical or material reality, but in some sphere of its own.

Similarly, the future also must exist in some way in a sphere of its own.

The "Eternal Now"

The key that the spiritual seeker possesses is the knowledge that the subconscious does not differentiate between past, present, and future, but is aware of all spheres of Time as part of the "Eternal Now."

At the same time we must learn to distinguish between certain kinds of precognitive experiences and to identify them as part of the normal processes of the subconscious.

A woman dreams of coming down with the measles and laughs it off. She did not succumb to the disease as a child, why should she weaken as an adult?

In two days she is in bed with the annoying rash covering her body.

Rather than judge this to be a prophetic dream, we might better regard the experience as an example of the subconscious mind being much more aware of the condition of the inner body than the superficial mind.

In other instances a keen intellect and a great awareness of one's environment will enable one to make predictions. Those men and women who have become affluent due to such diverse activities as stock market juggling or hemline raising have gained their wealth because of their abilities to assess the preferences of a mass society in alignment with cycles of past human enterprises and endeavors.

Pendragon on Prophecy and the Problem of Time

True power of prophecy rests not in some arcane and hidden knowledge but within the transcendent Self, which seems to be aware of events that belong in the realm of the future for the superficial Self.

The great contemporary British prophet, John Pendragon, once discussed the power of prophecy and the problem of Time in the following manner.

In my opinion, Time is a condition created by the mind while we are on earth so that we can appreciate space--Time and Space being, in normal conditions, interlocked.

Most people seem to imagine that events that lie in what we term the future are "fixed" on a sort of moving belt that we call Time, and that Time moves the event out of the future into the so-called present.

If they reflected for a moment, they would realize there is no such thing as present. Utter the word "present" or "now," and even as you utter it, part of the word has vanished into the past, while the part yet to be uttered is still a fraction of a second in the future. Nobody can isolate a point in time and say, "This is the present." It is rather like trying to define a point or a line as Euclid did--it isn't there.

It clearly seems, then, that Time has something to do with consciousness. Either an event has not happened yet or it has happened--at least that is how it seems while we are apparently naturally and normally "locked" in our bodies, never forgetting that man is *not* his body. Man's body is only a building that he is living in for a few score years.

If there is no present, how then is it that events are spaced out? If there is no present, then events must be either in the future or in the past. "Now" seems a very real thing to us. Nevertheless, even this illusive *now* has something queer about it. Sometimes *now* seems much longer than other times. The passage of Time is strangely elastic from the mind standpoint.

As a certain wit said, "When one is having a tooth drilled, a minute seems like an hour but when one has one's sweetheart on one's knees, an hour seems like a minute!"

The newborn and the senile have no conception of Time.

It is difficult even to attempt to conjecture on the

nature of Time, because one lacks an apt phraseology. Let me attempt to give my personal description.

Let us suppose that one has a very long table, and at intervals of two or three inches a small object has been placed. First, for example, a button, then a match box, a pin, a bead, and so on, until 50 or more objects have been spaced out down the table. Now the room is plunged into darkness.

A person who has no knowledge of the objects on the table enters the darkened room. (In effect, he is born.) He is handed a very tiny, low-powered flashlight with a beam sufficient to illuminate only *one object at a time.* He directs the beam on the first object--the button. The beam of light represents his consciousness. For a second, he recognizes and appreciates the object that he has illuminated. Then he moves the beam on to the second object, and at the same time, the first one "vanishes" into darkness again. Object one, by "vanishing," has moved into the past. Meanwhile, object two, being illuminated, is in the present, whereas object three and all subsequent objects are in the future.

Finally, after he has illuminated each object in turn, he reaches the last one, and his illumination--his conscious-ness, in a "beam sense"--goes out. (The moment of physical death.) Then somebody enters the room and switches on a big light over the table, and the examiner discovers that he can see *all* the objects at the same time. In short, his tiny beam of consciousness has been exchanged for a greatly enlarged one.

Fate and Free Will

Now I will attempt to give my personal opinions as to the nature of fate and free will.

As I said earlier, there are persons who vaguely imagine that events that lie in what we term the future are all fixed on a sort of moving belt called Time, and all we can do is to sit back and wait for the belt to move the event into the present.

I may be wrong, but long experience has shown me--or appears to show me--that the stuff (I cannot find a more apt word) of the future is plastic. It can be molded by thought. In short, it is *psychoplastic*.

If we hold a mind-picture for a long time, we tend to materialize it, especially if there is no doubt in our hearts and if we do not alter that picture. If we alter the picture or begin to doubt, we cannot bring what we desire out of the immaterial to the material. It is rather like getting a jelly to set. One must not stir it. The more powerful the thought and the sharper the picture, the more quickly we shall be able to materialize it.

Let me add that this technique is indeed a two-edged weapon, for it will work for both good and evil. In the latter, it is a case of "the thing I feared most has come upon me." The late Dr. Alexander Cannon, author or many works on the occult, told of a patient who was fearful of dying of a certain rare disease. She read everything that had been written about it, and daily dwelt upon her fear. In due time, she contracted the disease. *She had clothed her thought in matter*, but negatively so.

Thus it would seem that, to revert to the analogy of the moving belt called Time, it is possible to determine by voluntary action what sort of thing is to reach us on the belt. But we have to bear in mind that not one person in ten thousand makes a *deliberate technique* out of getting what they want. Life to them is mostly a variegated patchwork of events.

Changing Future Possibilities

It is possible to change the nature of what has been foreseen, but only by deliberate action. I recall reading of a case recently in which a woman dreamed she was in a car that had a tire blowout at a certain point on a cliff road. In the dream the car plunged over the cliff.

The day came when she was traveling in the car towards that point, but as the car neared the place where she had dreamed it would plunge over the cliff, the driver was ordered to slow down to three miles an hour. It was then that the car had the blowout--without falling to disaster over the cliff. Thus, it seems that what one "sees" as a "future event" may not necessarily be one, but the prediction is heeded and considered as a warning.

My own opinion is that fate operates rather like this:

A man may be fated to go from New York to San Francisco. This he is *fated* to do. There is no escape. He cannot go to any other destination. He must go to San Francisco.

The element of free will enters into the matter with regard to the mode and route of his journey. He can fly directly from New York, or he can go by rail or by road. If he chooses road, he can go by car or even by bicycle or on foot. He can go by sea, via the Panama Canal. He can go north and then west via Canada and then south again, or he can sail due eastward and approach San Francisco from the west. In the selection of a route he has choice, but in one thing he has no choice--his destination.

I think that in one or two things we are fated, but that in a vast number we have free will. Whatever route we decided to choose, however, we only choose it as another means of getting to our fated destination.

I have noticed, also, that those persons who govern nations are rather more fated than others. The same seems to apply to those whose life is involved with the guidance or service of large numbers of other persons.

Rising Above the Limitations of Physical Consciousness

One of our own favorite analogies that describes the true nature of Time has a man riding on the rear platform of a train. He looks to the left and to the right. As the train chugs along, he is able to see a panorama of new scenes as they come into view. As the train continues, these scenes fade into the distance and are lost to view. They have become his past.

However, the scenes do continue to exist after they have passed from the man's view, and they were in existence before he perceived them, even though he was only able to see them during the moments that they were his present.

At that same time, if another man were flying high above the train in an airplane, he would be able to see the train passenger's past and present, as well as future scenes that lie beyond the man's limited ground-level view. All would exist for the man in the airplane as an "Eternal Now."

It is the task of the spiritual seeker to rise above the accepted limitations of consciousness and to abide, at least for a time, in the Eternal Now.

Moving Through Time

Here is a simple exercise with which to begin to exercise your facility of moving through Time:

Sit quietly for a minute or two in a room of your house or apartment that contains a number of items or personal belongings that are especially meaningful to you.

Think next of all the activities or things that are happening in, around, and through you. Perceive how many realms of endeavor and existence in which you function daily.

See yourself at work, at leisure, at love.

See yourself interacting with the variety of men and women whose lives you touch each day.

Take some time to comprehend how many spheres of consensual reality with which you connect in the course of a 24-hour period.

Now project to the realities of your parents, your friends, or loved ones from whom you are separate. Understand in what way you are a part of their lives even though you are far removed from them in a geographical sense.

Do your best to perceive how each of these sovereign realities communicate with one another on some level of consciousness.

After you have done this for a time, begin to extend your awareness into the past.

Focus your attention on some object in the room that has been a part of your reality for a significant duration of time. Pick something that you have possessed for a long time. If someone owned it previously and gave it to you, that is even better.

How old is the object? From where did it come? How did it enter your life?

Imagine who made it. Imagine the materials from which it was made. Imagine their origins and how they blended to form the object you now possess.

Finally, turn your attention to what is possible for each thing on each happening. Explore the future potential of each reality.

How much can you perceive? How much can you imagine?

Attempt to get a true sense of the many realities in which you exist. Attempt to comprehend in how many ways these realities bend and flow with one another.

Looking Inside Other People's Skulls

Here is an exercise to practice while you are riding on a bus, an airplane, a commuter train, or while you are seated in a restaurant or some public place.

Look about you and perceive the other humans in your environment as five-dimensional shapes.

Imagine that you have the ability to visualize each person's activities as stretched out and as visible to your eyes. Imagine that you have the ability to perceive threads flowing from each individual and connecting themselves to their activities and experiences. Follow the threads and visualize each person's work, family, recreation, and so forth.

Next imagine that you can see inside people's skulls and perceive their brains as computers and television screens. Perceive each person's inner adventure and fantasies. Imagine each person's worries, plans, and dreams. Guess each person's strengths and admirable qualities.

Using the Past to Project into the Future

Another exploration into Time may be conducted alone in a quiet place with only you and a record player.

Put on a piece of music that is personally significant to you--one that is loaded with nostalgia or romance or unrequited love or a moment of great happiness.

Sit quietly and permit your thoughts to drift back to the time, the place, the happening when you first heard the music or when the music became personally significant for you.

Permit yourself to flow as completely back to the time, the place, the person as possible. Feel the emotions that you felt then. Remember details of clothing, weather, time of day, and so forth.

If that person is no longer with you, visualize where that person is now, what he or she is doing, feeling, and thinking. Imagine that you can establish a linkup on some level of consciousness with that person right now. Communicate a feeling; a sensation; an impulse of love, regret, forgiveness, goodwill, or whatever may be appropriate.

Now continue to follow the linkup into the future. Understand that you have the ability to connect yourself to this individual wherever he or she may be--even if they have passed to another dimension of reality.

See this individual as he/she will appear in the future. See the eyes, the mouth, the complete face.

Understand that you have the ability to communicate with that person on some level of consciousness. Know that you can make your presence and your thoughts felt on some level of awareness. Know that you have the ability to communicate a feeling of love, forgiveness, goodwill, appreciation or whatever impulse may be appropriate for that individual.

The Inner Reality of Dreams

In altered states of consciousness, such as dreams, hypnosis, or trance states, people may experience subjective realities much as they ordinarily would experience their existence in the external world. Even though the individual may recognize that the inner reality that is being experienced is internal, he may yet feel himself as participating with some or all of his senses in the subjective reality that is presently dominating his awareness.

Certain researchers have felt that one may best understand the experiencing of a subjective reality as a waking dream. In the altered state--however it is brought about--imagination is vivified to the extent that the person, usually with eyes closed, sees clearly the subjective reality, hears, touches, and is touched, is aware of moving about, and otherwise functions as people often do in dreams. Also, as in certain kinds of dreams, the person may be a spectator only, observing the subjective reality in a manner similar to experiencing a film in a theater.

When we gain access to our subjective realities, we open up an enormous number of possibilities for an enhancement of creativity, learning, and types of Self-expression conducive to healing and to personality development and integration. The more that we learn how to explore constructively our subjective realities, the more that we learn how to break out of the learned tyranny of Time.

Time Tripping Across the Universe to Receive Instruction from Great Teachers of the Future

As previously instructed in your "dream rehearsal," you may engage the assistance of a trusted individual to read the induction and the experiences to you, or you may previously record the instructions in your own voice.

Relax yourself completely. Let every muscle relax. Let your mind begin to drift and float.

Imagine that you are walking down a peaceful country lane toward a soft, green area of countryside. You know that this is a beautiful, tranquil place. You know that you will be safe and protected here. You know that this is a holy place, surrounded by the golden energy of unconditional love.

You find a lush, grassy area--a place that feels special and right to you--and you lie down. The grass is like a soft, fluffy blanket beneath you, and you nestle comfortably down into it.

You know that this is a perfect place to rest, to find peace, to enjoy nature. It is, oh, so lovely, so peaceful...so lovely, so peaceful.

Lie down, stretch out, and begin to take nice, long, deep breaths...nice, slow, deep breaths. Relax here in your grassy, soft bed. The sound of a nearby bubbling brook adds to the beauty of this place, this holy place. The trickling water lapping over the rocks will help to lull you to sleep.

As you lie on your back gazing upward, you notice that the sky is a clear blue...with fluffy, white clouds spotting it now and then.

Some of the clouds hang as if suspended. Some appear to be moving slowly across the arc of the blue, blue sky.

It is, oh, so peaceful, so wonderful. Relax, your body is falling asleep. You are becoming more and more relaxed, and you find yourself breathing deeper and deeper, slower and slower.

A fresh, cool breeze makes breathing so easy...and you find yourself breathing so easily. Your taut muscles expand and then gently relax. It is so peaceful, so wonderful, so soothing to lay here resting and watching the clouds. The breeze carries the faint, sweet fragrance of lilacs and a spring garden with a bouquet of aromas.

Your body responds to this peaceful, restful, holy place with a great desire to sleep. Your body is falling asleep...but your mind will remain aware.

The soothing, gentle warmth of an afternoon sun feels like loving, warm fingers, soothingly massaging the muscles of your body and helping you to fall asleep.

You can feel the soft, warm sun caressing, soothing, the muscles in your feet...your toes...your heels. The warm fingers are moving, massaging the muscles in your ankles...your calves... warming, soothing...relaxing all the muscles of your legs. Healing, soothing, warmth moves deep into your knees...your thighs...your hips...moving deep into the joints...healing, warming, releasing all tensions.

You are so relaxed, so peaceful, as the gentle, soothing warmth moves into your abdomen...deep into the lowest part of your back...into your chest...your shoulders...permitting all of your muscles to relax, all of your body to fall into a deep, deep sleep.

Nothing you hear will disturb you. Any sound that you might hear--a cough, a sniffle, a closing door, someone's voice--every sound and every movement that you hear will only help you drift into deeper and deeper sleep.

Now the soothing, gentle, warm fingers of the Sun slide up your spine. All tensions in your neck and scalp are relaxed and your body sleeps...your body sleeps. You are calm and at peace.

The warm, gentle fingers of the Sun gently massage the area above your ears, your temples...relaxing you completely ...letting all the muscles of the face relax...and fall asleep. Nothing can disturb you...nothing can distress you. You are at peace. You are at one with yourself.

You are growing in awareness that you possess free will...the choice to vibrate at a higher or lower frequency.

Even now, as you lie there in peace and tranquility, you are feeling the three highest vibrations of this plane of existence begin to enter your body. Feel now the beautiful vibration of Love move warmly through your body. Feel the gentle, electrical vibration of Wisdom move through your very essence. Feel the gentle, pulsating vibration of Knowledge move through your central Self. Feel your entire being vibrate with Love, Wisdom, and Knowledge.

You are seeing patterns of Time moving before you. You know that you now have the ability to move into the future. It does not matter from whence comes this ability, you know and understand that you have the power to see the future as it will be.

You are moving forward on the vibration of the Eternal Now. As you move forward in Linear Time, you are aware that Time is a great circle, a great spiral, not a straight line that moves inexorably from a near point to a distant point. As you move forward in Time, you are made aware that the Universe is conscious only to conscious humankind.

You now are approaching a city in future time (this should be wherever you wish it to be) wherein resides the great master teacher (create a name and a profession--physicist, author, chemist, etc.). The year is (whichever future time with which you wish attunement).

Visualize yourself walking through the streets of _____. Become fully aware of the environment.

What do you notice most about the city?

What do you observe about the methods of travel?

What most captures your attention about the buildings?

If there are men and women nearby, what do you most notice about them?

Now visualize yourself walking a path that will lead you to _____ (the Master Teacher). You are approaching the home or the spiritual retreat wherein resides the one whom you have moved forward in Time to visit.

Take a moment now to experience fully your emotions as you walk the path. Feel deeply and savor your expectations.

The Master Teacher whom you are seeking is said to be able to answer wisely any question that is put to him (her). You are pleased that you have received an invitation to visit the wise one and to ask about a matter that troubles you.

Now turn off the path and begin to approach the domicile of the master. Be aware of your inner thoughts and feelings.

Feel your knuckles touch the door. Understand your emotions as you await the opening of the portal and your signal to enter.

As a disciple or a student ushers you in, you are able to see an office, a study of the Future. You are able to see one in robes sitting near a communications device. You know that it is the wise one, the Master Teacher.

As you approach the Teacher, a student steps forward and brings about greater illumination in the study. As the lights become brighter, you're clearly able to see the Master Teacher.

Become totally aware of him (her).

See his clothes, his body, his face, his eyes, his mouth, the way he holds his hands.

He (she) gestures to you that you should be seated.

The Master Teacher nods to you, indicating that you may now ask a question that is important to you.

When you ask your question, notice how he will respond to your words. See how carefully he will listen. See how thoughtfully he will consider your question.

Continue to observe him closely.

He (she) may answer your question with a facial expression alone.

He may answer your question with a gesture of the hands or a shrug of the shoulders, or he may answer your question at some length with cautiously selected words.

He might even show you something; some object or symbol may appear in his hands.

Ask your question now. (*Pause 15 seconds.*)

What kind of reply does he give you?

What answer do you receive? (*Pause 15 seconds.*)

Be certain that you understand completely what he has said.

How do you feel about what he has said? Are you pleased with the answer?

How do you feel toward the Master Teacher?

The Wise One is indicating that you may ask another question if you so desire. If you wish, ask the Master Teacher another question, once again carefully observing the manner in which he answers. (*Pause 15 seconds.*)

Be careful again that you completely understand what the Master Teacher is telling you. (*Pause ten seconds.*)

A student steps forward and indicates that you must leave. The time allotted for your audience in the Future has passed.

Before you leave, speak to the Master Teacher, tell him anything that you want him to know. (*Pause ten seconds.*)

Now as you say good-bye, the Master Teacher reaches into his desk and brings forth a box. He tells you that he has a very special gift to present to you. He wishes you to take the object with you.

He opens the box and hands you the gift. Look at it. See what it is.

Tell the Master Teacher how you feel about him and about his gift. Say good-bye, for now you must leave.

As you walk down the path, your thoughts are on the Master Teacher, his answers to your questions, and the special gift he presented to you.

Once you are outside the gate of his home, open your hands and look at your gift once again in the moonlight. Turn it over in your hands. Smell it. Feel it. Discover all that you can about the gift.

Is there anything you notice that you overlooked when the

Master Teacher gave you the gift?

What deep significance does this gift have for you?

Know that you have the ability to use this gift wisely and to its most positive advantage.

Now begin walking the path, carrying your gift with you. Look at all things near the path very carefully. Look at all the things around you.

Be totally aware of your surroundings so that you will be able to find your way back to the Master Teacher from the Future whenever you want to visit him and gain from his wisdom.

Now, with the thoughts of the Master Teacher forever in your memory, with the true value of the gift forever impressed in your awareness, begin to return to full consciousness. At the count of five, you will awaken fully.

Chapter 10

Dream Lovers Can Come True!

Is it possible to eventually meet, in real life, the object of our affections, known to us previously only through the medium of the dream state?

For centuries man's love ballads have included a good many melodies whose lyrics tell of dream lovers, who, the songs promise, will one day materialize as lovers of warm and acquiescent flesh. According to some men and women, their real-life experiences substantiate the promises made by those romantic songs and prove that a seed of love planted in a dream can someday produce a mature and lasting relationship.

Occasionally, we have received case histories of certain individuals who claim to have been haunted by a dream lover for years, until, one day, the very image of their nocturnal mate appeared before them as a very real human being.

Fred A.'s adolescent love life, which like nearly every teenager's love life was fraught with emotional storms, was further complicated by a vivid dream that he had when he was 16.

He never had been far away from his parents' farm in Nebraska, but in his dream he was walking along a road that led to an old covered bridge that spanned a small creek.

It was a beautiful autumn day, and multicolored leaves lay piled everywhere. As he crossed the bridge, he could see an old stone farmhouse, quite unlike anything that one would find in Nebraska.

Boldly he entered the kitchen of the house, where he found a lovely young girl with long blond hair. She was dressed plainly, but she was possessed of a natural beauty that did not require the accentuation of elegant clothing. She smiled a warm, loving smile at Fred, then began to walk toward him, her softly curving hips moving sensuously under the fabric of her cotton dress.

"Because it was a dream," Fred A. noted with amusement,

> she walked right into my outstretched arms. It seemed as though we had known each other for years. We kissed; we hugged; we were delightedly happy in each other's arms. I called her by name, and she whispered my name over and over again.
>
> "Don't keep me waiting too long," she said, becoming anxious when I said that I must go. "I'll wait as long as I can, but don't keep me waiting too long!"

The dream left Fred feeling strangely warm and exhilarated. There was a girl waiting for him somewhere. What did pimples on his face and petty quarrels with the girls in his class matter now? Somewhere his true love waited for him.

But, at the same time, Fred felt terribly lonely. Where was the girl now, when he needed her? There were proms and picnics and dances to attend right then.

> I knew that I had to put the dream girl out of my mind. I dated a lot of really wonderful girls, but at the oddest and sometimes most inopportune moments, my thoughts flashed back to that beautiful dream image. In my dream I had said her name, but upon awakening, I could remember it only as something like "Brenda," but I knew that was not correct.

When World War II broke out, Fred enlisted and was sent overseas to England. "My dream went with me," he stated in an account of his dream lover that he prepared for interested researchers.

> I certainly did not lead a monklike existence, but while my buddies were forming steady relationships and

some were taking war brides, I found myself haunted by my dream mate.

How often did I argue with myself that I should marry some nice English girl rather than sit alone at night in the canteen, brooding over what may only have been the figment of some fantasy? Certain of my close friends began to wonder what was eating me, but I never dared to tell them. They probably would have had me out on a mental discharge.

Fred was discharged in 1945, and through a mix-up in his papers, found himself stranded in New York City for a few days. A buddy of his from Vermont invited him to spend the weekend at his folks' farm. After nearly four years in London, New York City held no big thrills for him, so Fred decided to accept his friend's offer. He had never seen a New England farm before, and a taste of rural living would help recondition him for Nebraska.

"It was my time for mix-ups, it seemed," Fred continued.

Jim's folks were supposed to pick us up at the bus depot, but when we arrived, there was no one there. Jim had left the message with his seven-year-old brother, and he feared that the word might not have been relayed to his parents. "It's only a couple of miles out of town," Jim grinned. "It's a beautiful day, and it might feel good to stretch our legs after that bus ride. Mind walking?"

The two ex-soldiers had not hiked far when Fred had the strangest feeling that he had walked along that country road once before.

Then they turned a corner, and he saw the old covered bridge that he had seen in that haunting adolescent dream. It was the same kind of startlingly lovely fall day, and the leaves were piled just as he remembered them.

I knew that around the next bend we would see that old stone farmhouse, but what I had not guessed was that the place would be Jim's home. He led me through the back door into the kitchen. My heart was thudding so hard that I thought I would faint. I knew *she* would be there in the kitchen, and *she* was.

An 18-year-old girl in a plain cotton housedress turned to smile at us from the sink where she was peeling potatoes. Her long blond hair swirled about her face as she ran to give Jim a warm kiss of welcome. "Hey, Fred," Jim laughed, freeing himself from the girl's embrace, "meet my kid sister, Brenna."
So it had been Brenna, not Brenda, Fred thought to himself. But he was too tongue-tied to say much of anything. The lovely blonde who stood before him, Jim's sister, was the girl of his dream.
"Brenna and I were in love before dinner that night," Fred concluded his account.

> I will always remember her first words of love to me: "Fred, darling, I've waited all my life for you." Today we are as much in love as we were on our honeymoon, and we have four children as physical proof of our love. I shall never be able to explain that remarkable dream. At the time that I first saw my "dream girl," she was only about 12 years old, yet I saw her as vividly as if she had been in the flesh, and just as she appeared on the day that I actually, physically, walked into her life.

Married in a Dream

A psychic told us of a handsome client of his who always had been extremely popular with the opposite sex, but who had reached the age of 33 with his bachelor status intact.
"I used to tease him," the psychic said.

> I used to ask him just what he was looking for. I would name each of the girls I had seen him with and enumerate all of their good points. Then I would challenge him to choose one of them for his wife. "No," he would tell me,

"somehow I will know when I have found the right girl. She will be the girl that I once married in a dream."

At last, almost overnight it seemed, the rascal got himself married. He called me from a nearby city and told me that he had not needed my psychic impressions about this girl. He had met her while on a business trip and had fallen instantly in love with her.

On the second day of their whirlwind courtship, he had said to her, "I know you. We were married in a dream that I had when I was 20."

The girl had replied, "And I know you. I had the same dream when I was 15. You were the groom, and I have been searching for you ever since."

There will be some who will say that such dreams are the result of the soul's yearning for its true Soul Mate, whose identity and whereabouts are known to the transcendent level of the unconscious mind. This information somehow manages to bubble up to the conscious mind during that altered state of consciousness we call dreaming. The image of the Soul Mate thereby becomes an object of idealized love to the dreamer, and he becomes obsessed with searching for the lover he has glimpsed in the shadow world of his dreams.

Others will inject elements from the reincarnation hypothesis into accounts of dream-lovers-come-true and will maintain that certain mates must be sought out in order that patterns of karma fruitfully may be played out.

Identifying Your Dream Lover
Through a Universal Time Scan

If you are willing to accept the past-lives hypothesis as a viable possibility--or even as an emotional exercise in attempting to identify your dream lover--the following process is a good one for stimulating memories and for prompting recognition of a potential mate or companion.

If for some reason you are recalling a past-life relationship, the following exercise will help you to learn why that memory is surfacing at this point in your life.

If you are projecting certain feelings toward a present-life friend, this technique will assist you in identifying the reasons why such emotions may be evolving.

If you are somehow envisioning a loving relationship with an individual whom you have not yet met in your presentlife experience, then this creative visualization will enable you to better deal with that provocative situation.

If your dream lover scenario somehow blends elements from each of the three possibilities listed above, then the following process is an excellent one by which those emotional strands might be lovingly woven together.

Follow the same procedures as instructed in the previous exercises in this book. Select one of the relaxation techniques that have been provided for you, permit yourself to relax as deeply and as completely as possible, and then listen to the voice of a trusted guide or your own pre-recorded instructions and openly explore the domain of your dream lover as it may exist in a Universal Time Scan.

Now that you are completely and totally relaxed, you will soon come into full awareness of scenes from past-life experiences about which you need to know for your good and your gaining.

You will be fully aware of what nations--as you understand them today--in which you achieved physical expression of your Soul. You will have full knowledge of the countries, places, or cities, as you would know them today.

You will have full knowledge of the time reference in which you lived. You will understand *when* you lived from the perspective of Time that you have today.

In each past-life scene that you will view, you will be aware of whether you are male or female.

You will be aware of your physical stature and proportions and you will have knowledge of your physical appearance.

You will know your ethnic group, the color of your skin, and your culture.

In each past-life scene you will be fully aware of any special circumstances regarding your physical body--whether or not you are crippled, blind, deaf, or handicapped physically in any way.

You will have complete knowledge of whether you were born into poverty, wealth, comfort or struggle.

A purple mist is moving up around you. It is the purple mist of Time. You know that you now have the ability to see and to scan all of Time. You will be able to feel which periods of Time attract you the most. You will be able to know in which segments of Time you lived.

You are moving back in Time. You are able to see all of Time as it swirls before you in a purple mist.

You are aware of your guide beside you, protecting you with the golden light of unconditional Love. You feel no fear as you move farther and farther back in Time.

You are seeing this nation when only the Red Man lived here. You see scattered villages on riverbanks, tall grasses, buffalo, deer.

Did you once live in those villages?

You are seeing Europe as it once was very long ago, when it was only villages, fortresses, and clustered cities on riverbanks...when it lived in fear of the sword, darkness, and the devil...when the lord and his knights from the castle on the hill were protector, judge, and jury.

Did you live then?

There is ancient Rome, the Eternal City. Did you stand on a street corner watching the mighty legions returning with yet another victory for Caesar?

See ancient Greece: Athens, Sparta, philosopher-kings, poet-warriors, odysseys through unknown lands. Did you partake of the drama and the glory that was Greece?

Soar to the walled cities of Peru, high in the Andes Mountains. Travel to the sprawling jungle empires of Mexico; stand on the shore of a placed called Atlantis.

Did you watch any of those once-great empires crumble into oblivion, topple into the sea, or perish under the sword of invading armies?

Look at the forgotten cities in Africa, populated by proud black men and women.

See the thriving culture in China before there was the Great Wall.

Stand on a fishing boat and look toward the shore of ancient

Japan and see the majestic cities.

Did you ever call any of those places "home"?

You have the ability to see all of Time. You have the ability to relive scenes from any prior life experience about which you need to know for your good and your gaining.

You have the ability to begin to move toward a particular scene from a particular past life about which you need to learn more information in order to help you identify a Lover who has come to you in your dreams.

A Scene From a Past Life in Which You Devoted Your Life to Spiritual Service

You are seeing yourself in a beautiful garden of contemplation or, perhaps, a majestic temple of worship. Take a moment to experience fully your emotions as you remember this place of spiritual significance.

Look carefully at your surroundings. What is there about the immediate area that most captures your attention, that most jogs your memories?

You see someone approaching you. You know that it is your Teacher from that life experience. See the love in those eyes as your Teacher sees you. Look deeply into those eyes, and remember the name of your Teacher.

Become totally aware of your Teacher. See your teacher's clothes, body, face, mouth, the way your Teacher walks and stands.

The scene that you are remembering is one in which your Teacher gave you an important awareness, a vital teaching, a lesson that you will be able to use to great advantage in your present life as well as that past life.

Observe your Teacher closely. The awareness may be transmitted by a facial expression alone or by a gesture of the body.

The Teacher may relay the teaching at some length with carefully selected words.

The Teacher may show you some object or symbol.

However the Teacher transmits the awareness, the lesson will tell you what you need to know in order to develop your spiritual abilities. The Teacher is giving you that vital teaching now.

Now that you have received once again that important aware-ness, look deeply into the eyes of your Teacher and see if you have come together again in your present-life experience. See and know if it has been your Teacher who has been visiting your dreams as a Divine Lover.

See if you have come together again to complete a lesson left unlearned, to finish some work left undone.

Look into the eyes, and for your good and your gaining, you will know.

The purple mist of Time swirls around you again, and you are witnessing yourself in a scene from another past-life experience. You are viewing yourself in a scene from a past life in which you had to struggle against great odds in order to achieve a meaningful goal.

Nothing you see will disturb you. Nothing will distress you. Everything that you see will be for your good and your gaining. You will be able to see everything from a detached and unemotional point of view.

You may be seeing yourself in a work situation, a political situation, or you may even be seeing yourself in a war, but you are seeing the scene clearly. You are detached, unemotional, but you are clearly seeing how you had to struggle against great odds in order to achieve a meaningful goal.

You are now looking into the eyes of a friend, a parent, or a lover--one who supported you in your great struggle.

These are the eyes of one who never failed you.

There are the eyes of one who always was there to comfort you, to hold you, to give you hope and courage to go on struggling.

Become totally aware of this loved one who meant so much to you in that past-life experience.

See the loved one's clothes, body, face, mouth, the movements of the loved one's body.

Take a moment to experience fully your emotions as you once again find yourself in the presence of this friend, parent, or lover.

You can see everything around you very clearly. Know and understand exactly where you are.

What is there about this place that most captures your attention?

For your good and your gaining, see if that friend, that parent, that lover has come with you in your present-life experience to complete a lesson left unlearned, to finish work left undone. Look into the eyes and you will know.

Now you are looking into the eyes of one who steadfastly *opposed* you in that lifetime of struggle and conflict.

These are the eyes of one who tried to block everything that you attempted. These are the eyes of one who sought to destroy your every effort toward your goal.

Become totally aware of this person who opposed you. See your antagonist's clothes...body...face...mouth...personal gestures and mannerisms.

Take a moment to see everything around you very clearly as you once again encounter this one who so opposed you. Know and understand where this encounter took place and why it took place.

See clearly whether or not you won or lost this vital personal conflict.

Now, looking deeply into the eyes of the one who opposed you, see if that person has come with you in your present-life experience to complete a karmic lesson left unlearned, to finish karmic work left undone. Look into the eyes and you will know.

The purple mist of Time comes around you once more, and you are being taken to a scene from a past life in which you had very special abilities, in which you had star power, in which you may have performed miracles.

See clearly what special ability you enjoyed in that past-life experience. Know if you had the ability to heal, to move objects with the mind, to levitate the physical body, to gain impressions of people and events far away, to gain glimpses of the future.

See clearly the place in which you most often performed your miracles, your special abilities.

What is there about this place that most captures your attention? What was there about this place that made it a favorite area for you?

You are seeing now the Spiritual Alchemist from that past life who most helped you to develop control of your special ability. Become totally aware of this person...the clothes...body...face...eyes...

mouth...the way the Spiritual Alchemist walks and moves the arms and hands.

You are remembering the day when you received your initiation from the Spiritual Alchemist. You will remember that the Spiritual Alchemist gave you a very special gift,an object that also will give you great assistance and comfort in your present-life experience.

Take a moment to remember the place in which you received initiation. Experience fully your emotions as you received the initiation.

Now recall how, as you were saying good-bye, the Spiritual Alchemist reached into a robe and brought forth a golden box. The Spiritual Alchemist told you that there was a very special gift for you in the box. The Spiritual Alchemist wanted you to take the object with you, to always carry the object with you.

Remember now as the Spiritual Alchemist opens the box and hands you the gift. Look at it. See what it is. Take the gift. Feel it. Know it. Understand fully how this gift can aid you greatly in solving problems in your present-life experience.

The purple mist of Time swirls around you once again, and you now are remembering a past-life experience when you gloried in a great and meaningful love.

This was a past-life experience in which you fully and completely understood the deepest depths and the farthest reaches of a great love relationship.

This was a past life in which you had a loved one at your side who always was there for you, faithful and loyal.

You slowly are becoming aware of the features of this great love as you sense someone moving toward you from the shadows. You are aware that this person whom you loved so dearly is moving toward the light, moving toward you.

You know that when the light begins to touch the loved one, you once again will perceive the features of your Soul Mate, one who has been with you in many lifetimes.

The light is first touching the top of the hair. See what color it is and how it is worn.

The light is now touching the eyes. See their color and their shape. Look deeply into those loving eyes and feel the adoration that flows to you from those beautiful eyes.

Now the light is caressing the face, chin, mouth, the neck. You remember all these marvelous features.

Take a moment to experience fully your emotions as you once again find yourself in the presence of this greatest of loves.

See clearly your Soul Mate's personal gestures and mannerisms, the way your beloved is dressed, the way your loved one moves.

As you stand there feeling the memory of love swelling within you, behold the entire form and structure of your Soul Mate, your Dream Lover. Know that love, like a golden cord, has stretched across Time and Space and brought your Soul Essences together again.

Go to your loved one. Feel those arms move around you again in a loving embrace. Feel those lips touch yours softly again in a kiss of joyous greeting and deepest love.

This is the one who always was there for you...always at your side...always ready to take up your cause against whatever foe might seek to confront you.

This is the Soul Mate who never sought anything other than what is best for you...for the two of you...for the One of you.

You now are becoming aware of a specific time and place in which you and your Dream Lover shared a particularly significant moment.

You have the ability to see clearly what dramatic or important action you two shared. You have the ability to remember in what time reference this deed took place and in what place or country it occurred--as you would recognize it today.

At the count of three, you will remember all these details clearly. **One**: coming clearer; **Two**: clearer still; **Three**: you see everything clearly now. (*Pause for 15 seconds.*)

Look deeply into the eyes of your Soul Mate. Know and understand what spiritual energy binds the two of you together. Know and understand if you once again very soon will meet your Soul Mate in the flesh.

Know and understand if your Soul Mate is to serve as a guide for you in your dreams, leading you to greater awareness and even deeper lessons of love from the soul plane of existence. Look into your Soul Mate's eyes, and you will know.

The purple mist of Time swirls around you to take you to the memories of a past life in which you were keenly aware of your extraterrestrial origin.

This lifetime may have occurred on Earth, or it actually may have been lived on some other planet. Wherever it occurred, you remember it clearly. Take a moment now to experience fully your emotions as you are walking in the environment of that lifetime.

What plants do you see around you? Are there any animals in sight? What are the main types of buildings in your vicinity?

Look up at the sky. See it by daylight. Now see it by night. Observe any constellations you might see.

What is there about this particular past-life environment that most captures your attention?

Now you are looking into the eyes of one with whom you shared a most important mission in that life experience. Become totally aware of this person, your partner. Know the clothes, body, face, mouth, and mannerisms of this person.

You are remembering a scene from that life experience in which your partner is describing to you the single most important element in your mission.

Observe your partner closely. Your partner may illustrate this element with a gesture of the body or by showing you some object or symbol. Your partner may describe the important element at length with carefully selected words. However your partner responds, it will be for your good and for your gaining. The information about your mission will be found to be vital in your present-life experience. Your partner is transmitting the information **now**. (*Pause for 20 seconds.*)

Now, filled with these awarenesses of your Dream Lover, your Soul Mate, you are coming back to full wakefulness. At the count of five, you will know those things about your Dream Lover that you are to remember for your good and your gaining. **One**: coming awake, filled with love; **Two**: coming awake feeling very good in body, mind, and spirit; **Three**: filled with new insights about your Dream Lover; **Four**: more and more awake; **Five**: wide awake and feeling great!

Analyzing Your Ideal Mate

Before you invest a great deal of time and energy searching your dreams or your past or present life experiences for your Soul Mate, it is a good idea to spend some time assessing what traits you really cherish in an ideal mate.

There are a number of devilishly clever stories about men and women who became ensnared in hellish marriages or tormented love affairs due to their own making--simply because they placed an incorrect emphasis on the more superficial qualities of the opposite sex. You may have read some of these moral parables or seen them enacted on such television shows as "The Twilight Zone." They always make for enthralling dramas, for they never fail to have a "snapper" ending wherein the incautious romantic finds himself or herself forever trapped in a love nest that turns out to be lined with emotional barbed wire.

The authors can speak from painful experience in this regard. After five-year-old Brad underwent a mystical interaction with a multidimensional entity, he was given Sherry's image to guide him to his Soul Mate. Because he did not take the time to employ such an extensive analysis as the following, he was terribly mislead by an image that deceived him into mistaking a counterfeit for the genuine. While Sherry was still in a nonphysical dimension, she was shown an image of Brad as a small boy; but she, too, was misled by someone who resembled him--and may even be distantly related to Brad.

We cannot emphasize strongly enough that as you utilize the following analysis you are certain that you have as many things as possible in common with your Soul Mate. Remember, your Oneness through eons of Time is what has brought you together again.

Wait until you know that you will have at least an hour of uninterrupted time, then sit for a few moments in reflective reverie before answering the following questions as honestly as possible.

After you have completed these questions for personal evaluation, refer to them from time to time. Devote very serious thought to patterns of your personality and/or that of your ideal mate or lover that may clearly emerge. Some day--we hope very soon

--when you have found the person you consider to be your Dream Lover, your Soul Mate, your most significant other, it would be an extremely good idea to have your beloved answer the questions so that you may compare notes before you set the wedding date!

What are your earliest memories of feeling an attraction toward a member of the opposite sex? _____

_____

What was it that attracted you to that particular person? _____

_____

_____

What sounds, odors, tastes, touch sensations, and mental images are associated with this memory? _____

_____

Holding these memories and feelings in your mind, reflect upon which member of the opposite sex has most attracted you during the past few days or weeks. _____

Who was the adult member of the opposite sex that you most admired in your childhood
        before you started elementary school? _____
        in grade school? _____
        in high school? _____
        college? _____

Now list the adult member of the opposite sex that you *disliked* most during those same stages.
        childhood _____
        high school _____
        college _____

Throughout your past, with whom do you feel you got along better --your father or your mother? _____

With whom do you feel you get along better today? _____

Describe the kind of person of your own sex with whom you seem to get along better. _____

Describe the kind of person of the opposite sex with whom you seem to get along better. _____

Name the person of your own sex that you feel has had the greatest influence upon your life. _____

Name the person of the opposite sex that you feel has had the greatest influence upon your life. _____

What do you consider to be your greatest personal problem in dealing with a member of the opposite sex? _____

Why do you believe that you have this problem? _____

Has a member of the opposite sex ever humiliated you or forced you to feel inferior? _____

Have you ever felt ashamed of an action or a statement that you have directed toward a member of the opposite sex? _____

What is your true basis for liking someone of either sex?

Wat is your true basis for disliking someone of either sex?

How important to you is physical attractiveness in a prospective mate or lover? _____

Do you make an effort to make yourself attractive to the opposite sex? _____

How important to you is intelligence in a prospective mate or lover? _____

How high would you rate your own intelligence? _____

During moments of introspection, have you discovered an infe-riority complex or any other defense mechanism within yourself?
_____

As you sit here in the privacy of your own personal examination, what opinions or beliefs do you hold about the opposite sex that you realize in honest introspection are probably irrational preju-dices? _____
_____

In interacting with members of the opposite sex, what kind of person will most
          amuse you? _____
          antagonize you? _____
          disgust you? _____
          create feelings of sympathy in you? _____
          arouse feelings of admiration in you? _____

How important to you is it that your prospective mate or lover share the same viewpoints regarding
          religion? _____
          politics?_____
          morality? _____
          ethics? _____
          social sensitivity? _____

Do you believe that happiness and/or love come more readily from Self-centeredness or from unselfishness? _____
_____

In all honesty, what really makes you happy? _____
_____

What is your basic philosophy about
    the quality or inequality of the roles of husband and wife?
    _____
    responsibility for the children? _____
    the disciplining of children? _____

Do you believe that you have the freedom to shape your own
destiny?_____

Do you think it is possible for a person to change his/her emotional
nature or basic behavior patterns? _____

Have you discovered from personal and specific experiences that
friends and loved ones change? _____

Do you ever feel lonely in a crowd or unhappy during moments
when you should be experiencing happiness? _____

Have you ever found yourself in a truly embarrassing social situation with a member of the opposite sex? _____

How would you say you handled yourself in that situation?
_____

Have you ever learned to your great dismay that you were inadequate in a situation with a lover or mate when you so very
much wished to be especially competent? _____

How did you respond to the situation? _____
_____

How did your companion respond to the situation and to your
efforts? _____

Do you often feign sophistication that you know that you truly do not possess? _____

What do you feel are your most desirable character traits? _____

_____

_____

What character traits do you most desire in a lover or mate?

_____

How important to you is intimate physical contact--kissing, hugging, petting? _____

How important to you is sex? _____

Would you ever demand sex if your partner was unwilling to participate?_____

Describe your ideal sexual relationship--frequency, type of love-making, etc. _____

In the privacy of your introspection, are there any ethnic groups toward which you feel a prejudice? _____

From what ethnic group would you most desire your ideal lover or mate to be a member? _____

What are your preferences for
     color of hair? _____
     color of eyes? _____
     height?_____
     weight?_____
     age?_____
     basic physical form or structure? _____

Would you accept a mate or lover who had a minor disease or physical deformity? _____

Would you accept a mate or lover who suffered from a serious disease or an accident or wound that was crippling or made the person conspicuous? _____

How important is it to you to be in control of a situation? _____

_____

How important is it to you to always do your best? _____

_____

How important is it to you to always be right or to win an argument?

_____

Have you ever harmed yourself by your own stubbornness or unwillingness to yield your point of view or position? _____

With which social classes are you most comfortable? _____

_____

What occasional or professional backgrounds do you know best?

_____

From which social class should your prospective or ideal companion issue? _____

What should be his/her occupational or professional background?

_____

What is your basic attitude toward money? _____

_____

Should your Dream Lover have the same philosophy toward money? _____

Where would you like to live with your Soul Mate? _____

_____

What single thing could your Dream Lover do or say that would truly make you the happiest? _____

_____

Chapter 11

Some Final Advice and Reminders

"We should neither be frightened by nightmares of pain nor unduly elated by dreams of beautiful experiences," Paramahansa Yogananda once remarked.

By dwelling on these inevitable dualities...of maya [the world of illusion], we lose the thought of God, the Changeless Abode of Bliss. When we awaken in Him we shall realize that mortal life is only a picture made of shadows and light, cast on a cosmic movie screen.

As we frequently have reminded you in this book, dreams speak to us in another language, that of parable and paradox, allegory and poetry, symbols and pictorial metaphors. Consequently, to receive the very most from your dream teachings, it truly behooves you to do the very best to learn to speak the language of dreams. Of course, we specifically mean *your* dreams.

In *The Meaning of Dreams*, psychologist Calvin S. Hall of the Institute of Dream Research in Santa Cruz, California, warns us that analyzing an isolated dream and attempting to draw major conclusions from it can be very misleading. Hall recommends that it is by studying a series of dreams, each related to the others "like chapters of a novel," that we can gain useful insights into our underlying conflicts. Continued analysis along these lines also may provide us with a greater perception of how we truly view the world--an awareness that may not be so apparent to us in our everyday waking life.

We quite agree with Dr. Hall and we underscore our advice that no matter how many dream dictionaries you might consult, you always will gain the most meaningful insights by your taking the time to learn the dream vocabulary most unique to you. Only you can truly tell if your dreaming of that flashy red sports car was truly just that--a dream of a red sports car--or if the automobile represented something else to you in your personal cosmology.

After you have worked with your dreams for quite a while and have developed a feel for your personal symbols, it would be most helpful to you if you compiled your own dream dictionary. One of the greatest aids to the personal exploration of your inner Self and your dream teachings would be your studying various symbol representations from other cultures--ancient and modern--as well as their myths, legends, and folklore. It is within such a heritage of humankind that you will begin to recognize which symbols in your dream dramas are universal and which are uniquely your own.

Preparing Your Dream Notebook

1. As has been stated often throughout this book, keep a journal, a notebook, a pad of paper and a pen or pencil by your bedside. Of course, we must add that in this age of gadgets and technological aids, some folks prefer a tape recorder at bedside or both a recorder and a note pad.

2. It is helpful to record the dates--day, month, year--in advance of your blinking into consciousness to write things down after waking from a dream. (Or you might buy a diary or journal with the dates already printed neatly there for you.) Having each entry dated will quite likely be important to you later in chronologically understanding the evolution of dream patterns. Dated entries also are necessary for the documentation of prophetic or warning dreams.

3. Remember lovingly and gently throughout the day to remind yourself that you will remember your dreams.

Re-remind or suggest the command to yourself: "I will remember my dreams!" after you have gone through one of the relaxation exercises before falling asleep.

4. Entering the relaxed state referred to previously is extremely important. Take some deep, slow breaths and tell yourself that you are relaxed, that you will have the kind of dream teachings that you most require, and that you will remember all that you need to remember for your good and your gaining.

Avoid sleeping pills, alcohol, or drugs. Research demonstrates that REM activity is greatly reduced after imbibing or ingesting any of the above.

Enhancing Your Ability to Dream

Dr. Henry Reed, of the Association for Research and Enlightenment and editor of *The Sundance Community Dream Journals*, suggests the Tibetan technique of focusing the desire for dreams into a concentrated "glow" in the back of the throat.

Some researchers say that dreams are more intense or easily remembered by taking a dose of vitamin B-6 or B-12 before going to sleep.

Recording Dreams

1. When you awaken during the night or first thing in the morning, record what you can remember of the dream. This can be done with *key words*.

You also might add a sketch or a drawing of your dream. Don't forget to draw and to identify any symbols that you deemed important.

Be certain to note in your dream diary the details of any feelings that were associated with the dream scenario (fear, elation, sorrow) and any physical results (sweating, trembling, crying out).

2. Taking a few moments for a brief time of stillness before you arise might help you to recall any significant dream information. A morning meditation also might be very helpful in drawing back dream imagery.

Throughout the day it is common to have mini-flashes from your dream teachings. Make notes of these, and record them in your dream journal as soon as you can.

3. If you should awaken in the middle of a dream and wish

to continue it, you can give yourself the suggestion to do so. This may take some practice, but it is not at all rare to develop such an ability.

4. If a dream troubles you or if you do not understand it, ask yourself to repeat the dream before going to sleep and request additional information that will be helpful in granting you a more complete understanding of the teachings received.

William Benton Clulow, an English clergyman of the early nineteenth century, once remarked that nothing convinced him more of the boundlessness of the human mind than its activities in dreaming.

Frederick Henry Hedge, an American cleric of the same period, expressed his sentiments toward dreaming in these words: "Dreaming is an act of pure imagination, attesting in all men a creative power, which, if it were available in waking, would make every man a Dante or a Shakespeare."

It is our contention that we gain ready access to enormous, untapped powers of mind through the agency of dreams. The dream teachings that can transform us into Shakespeares, Einsteins, Mozarts--and any other acme of artistic or intellectual perfection that we can name--are available to each of us without cost. We have but to lie down in peaceful slumber and permit our psyches to achieve an attitude of openness to the Blessed Harmony that governs the Universe.

Appendix
Dream Dictionary

We have included a dream dictionary in this book with the admonition that you use it only as an aid to assist you in forming your own personal lexicon of dreams, for only that which is truly your own will be the one that will have any real meaning for you.

Please first try your very best to determine what the symbols revealed in your dreams mean to you as an ever-evolving, everlearning spiritual entity. If you really seem to be stuck over a particular bit of symbology, then use our dictionary as a reference tool, a catalyst in helping you to divine the meaning of that troublesome imagery. Our dream dictionary should only be utilized as a kind of mental trigger to fire your own thoughts into full realization.

Accident--Warning to beware of danger; may be precognitive of literal accident. Freudian implications related to sex or hostility. An accident at sea may pertain to love affairs; on land, business affairs.

Accounting (keeping books)--Related to one's karma, the debits and credits of life. It also can refer to a monotonous life pattern that needs change.

Acrobat--Overcoming life's problems. Tightrope walker denotes walking a precarious line. Heading for a fall or perhaps taking a great leap.

Adam--Instinctive man. Nature. Strength.

Adultery--If not literal, perhaps it refers to hidden guilt or a desire for something not in your best interest or that of others.

Age or Aged--Your wiser Self, the Higher Self. A fear of growing older.

Airplane--Soaring spiritual attitudes.

Alien--Feelings of isolation, of being different. Important changes are coming.

Alley--The past. Something away from the beaten path. A short-cut to something, but not necessarily the best route to the goal. A secret, sometimes of a sordid nature.

Alligator--A crafty nature. Danger from an unsuspected area.

Altar--The level of Inner Awareness. Spiritual values. A sacrifice.

Anchor--Tied down. Desire to settle down. Power from deep within.

Angel--Contact with Higher Self or superconsciousness. Teacher. Messenger. Guidance. Wisdom. Truth.

Ankh--The mystery of Egypt. Eternal life.

Apple--If the dreamer is fundamental in religious thinking, it could represent a fall from spirituality. Desire. Hunger for knowledge. If ripe or sweet--omen for rewards. If green or bitter--loss or danger through foolishness.

Armor--Protection. Self-defense. Rigidity.

Ashes--A burned-out love. Remember the phoenix--a new beginning from the ashes.

Athlete--Physical attributes. Running from a problem.

Attic--Part of the "house" or yourself. Reaching for higher attainment at the spiritual level; if it is empty, it needs filling. A secret attainment.

Authority Figure--Whether a king, president, or teacher, it generally represents one's Higher Self.

Autumn--The latter years of one's life. Accomplishment, fulfillment. Too late.

Baby--New concepts, ideas. Happiness. Responsibility. Infantile emotions.

Back Door--Looking back. Past problems. Karma.

Baldness--If not a warning (literally), could refer to truth. Seeing people as they really are, not as they prefer you to see them.

Balloon--Spiritual elevation. Out-of-body experience. Fantasy.

Bandage--Something to hide a hurt (emotional). Approaching injury.

Bank--A storehouse; prestige. Abundance of love. Desire for wealth. A safe place to hide.

Banquet--Emotional need for love. A desire to overindulge.

Barber--Freudian castration symbol; loss of strength or manhood (womanhood).

Basement--The Self; the level of the subconscious mind.

Bathing--Spiritual cleansing. Need to "clean up" your life.

Battle--Opposing ideas. Conflict within.

Beach--If the sea covers the beach, a death wish. Calm sea: peace and serenity.

Bear--This animal may indicate a distrust of the opposite sex. Possessiveness. Father symbol. Stocks and bonds. Nudity. (American Indian medicine interpretation: A family-centered individual, a devoted lover, someone who has great, silent strength.)

Beaver--Indicates the necessity for putting all your effort into a project. "Work like a beaver."

Bees--Much activity. Busy. Do not get "stung" on a deal. (American Indian medicine interpretation: An industrious, selfless, Self-sufficient person who can deal with a wide range of activities.)

Beggar--Dependence on others. Rejection. Depression. Spiritual seeking.

Bells--Marriage, funeral, church? Can be a joy or sadness related to other parts of the dream.

Bicycle--Activity, sexual or spiritual. If riding uphill: frustration.

Bird--Freedom of the Soul. A messenger. (American Indian medicine power: A bird sitting in a tree represents one who has high ideals, who finds places of trust and integrity.)

Birth--Fear or joy, depending on your own thoughts about the subject. New ideas.

Blindness--Symbolic of one's inability to "see" or understand clearly.

Boat or Ship--Out-of-body experience. One's Self, sailing along the sea of life.

Books--Hidden knowledge. May refer to past lives and karma. Need for knowledge.

Boss--An authority figure, the Higher Self.

Bottle--Emotional concealment. Male symbol (Freudian). If full: prosperity; if empty: loss.

Box--Same as bottle, but Freudian female symbol. That which holds in, protects.

Bread--Kindness, love, or poverty, depending on other symbols present. Basic sustaining life focus.

Bride--Fulfillment; hope.

Bridesmaid--Frustration. Failing to achieve a desired goal.

Bridge--Crossing from one way of life to another, hopefully better.

Broom--Cleansing; cleaning away old problems or karma.

Brother--A bond. Spiritual brother. Another part of your Self.

Buffalo--A symbol of great force and strength.

Bullfighting--Freudian symbol for hatred of one's father. Stock market concern.

Butcher--An unconscious fear of either sex. Freudian castration symbol. Be cautious about being tricked--"butchered."

Butterfly--Success. Happiness. A rebirth experience. (American Indian medicine: Peaceful conditions are moving steadily forward.)

Cake--A celebration. Reward.

Cancer--Generally denotes a hidden warning about something. Spiritual erosion.

Cane or *Crutch*--Dependency on something or someone.

Car--Freudian for body. Jungian for drive, determination. The vehicle with which we move through life.

Cat--Universal symbol for woman. May refer to gossip; beware of gossip. The mysterious. Independence. Sexuality. (American Indian medicine interpretation: Suspicion. A person whose outward show of calm may shatter at any time.)

Cave--The subconscious mind. Freudian for womb. Protection from worldly events. Hidden.

Choke--To choke someone is a release of hostility. Being choked may indicate current problems that seem insurmountable.

Christ--The Higher Self-Contact with Superconscious Mind.

Christmas--To the Christian this refers to great love; a time of fulfillment. Expectation. Throughout the Western world, a time of joy, of giving and receiving.

Church--The realm of Inner Awareness. Higher Self. Spiritual need. Safety.

Circle--Wholeness. Integration. Eternity.

Circus--Activity. Elation, joy. Longing to return to childhood.

Classroom or *School*--Learning; life's lessons.

Climbing--Spiritual attainment. Reaching for higher spiritual values. To Freud, like most symbols, it related to sexual activity.

Clock--Common to those fearing death. Time is running out, etc. A symbol of the material world, as opposed to the "timelessness" of the spiritual planes.

Closet--The subconscious mind. One's Inner Self. Secret thoughts. If empty: in debt; if full: profit.

Coat--Security, love, protection. Attitudes.

Coffin--Anxiety symbol. Death of an idea or emotion. Literally could foretell physical death, but usually is symbolic.

College or *University*--The School of Life symbol. Knowledge.

Convent--Withdrawal from life. Spiritual service to others.

Cook--Giving to others. Love. Food of life.

Courtroom--Justice or injustice. Guilt-consciousness.

Criminal--Payment of karmic debt or person paying karmic debt.

Cripple--An emotional cripple. Needing assistance.

Cross--Christ Consciousness. Spiritual illumination. Protection.

Crowd--The many facets of one's personality.

Crying--Emotional release, as in the conscious state.

Dagger--Betrayal; hatred; Freudian phallic symbol.

Dancing--Happy association. Sexual activity.

Darkness--The lack of spiritual light. Insurmountable problem.

Dead--Emotional death, not physical. (Physical death often denoted by dreams of travel, unless travel is a normal part of your life.)

Desert--Spiritual thirst. Emotional barrenness. Lack. Sterility.

Devil--Unpleasant person. Authoritarian figure of negative emotions. Parent figure for unhappy childhood. Search for forbidden knowledge.

Diamonds--Purity symbol. Wealth. Wedding. Truth.

Dinosaur--You are about to bring forth new ideas from the old. If the giant creature is silent or threatening, your new concepts may not be readily accepted.

Dirt--Worry about what others might think. Guilt.

Disease--Uneasy; dis-ease. Unconscious fears. Unworthiness.

Doctor--One who inflicts pain or one who saves lives. Desire for healing. Correction of errors.

Dog--Faithfulness or vicious enemy, depending on your like or dislike for dogs. Friend or foe. (American Indian medicine: Devotion. A friend who is always available when truly needed.)

Doll--Fear of being controlled by others.

Door--Open: opportunity; closed: lost opportunity.

Doves--Peace or hope.

Dragon--Repressed emotion. Subconscious power. Materialism.

Dress--New aspect in your life, physical or spiritual. Self-identity.

Drinking--Love. Pure water denotes a spiritual cleansing. Fizzy, bubbly: excitement; sweet: love.

Drowning--Difficulties in your life, problems that seem beyond hope. Possessive love. Unconscious death wish. Need rescuing.

Drunkenness--A wish to escape responsibility. An abundance of love, life, and desire--eat, drink, and be merry.

Duck--A symbol of one who is a friend to all creatures (American Indian medicine interpretation).

Dueling--Inner conflict. A contest; argument.

Dwarf--Looking down upon someone, or feeling someone is looking down on you. A feeling of insecurity.

Earth--The Earth Mother. "Down to earth."

Earthquake--Inner turmoil. Old ideas and problems coming forth. Literal or prophetic. Changes.

Eating--Love fulfillment; if pleasant, food, or opposite if not a food the dreamer cares for. Escaping problems, as in conscious state.

Eel--This is an ancient Chinese symbol for fertility, signalling pregnancy. Can refer to such matters as saving money (building a "nest egg," etc.). New life.

Egypt--Mystery. Magic. Being set free from old worries and responsibilities.

Elder Brother--The Higher Self or wiser part of Self. Spiritual teacher.

Elephant--Denotes a large capacity for work or a long memory. Power.

Elimination--A psychological, physical, or emotional cleansing is indicated.

Engineer--An authority figure, often associated with the Higher Self or God.

Eve--Anima figure. Temptress. Nature.

Exam--Life test. Fear of failure.

Executioner--Hidden guilts; Self-punishment. Unconscious hostility.

Eye--The Eye of God. The ego. Self-examination needed. Keep alert.

Falling--A natural fear and common to children. Falling from grace or higher spiritual realms. Fear of karmic setback. Defeat. Out of control.

Farm--Return to the earth. Abundance. Peace and plenty. Independence.

Father--If not literal, authority figure. Depends on your past relations with your own father, whether pleasant, sad, or fearful. Higher Self or God. Astral travel.

Fat Person or *Fat Self*--Emotional bigness. Joy. Burdens in life. Contentment.

Faults of Another--Usually symbolize one's own faults looked at objectively.

Feather--To find a feather in your dream is to find a symbol that you will soon receive good news (American Indian medicine symbol).

Feet--Understanding, freedom, or exposure of one's thoughts and ideals.

Fence--"Fenced in." Barrier. Protection.

Fiddle--Wasting your time or your life. Love of music. Sexual dalliance.

Field or *Open Space*--Wandering aimlessly. Lost feeling. Undecided.
Fire--Literal at times, but usually refers to emotional state--"fired up." Enthusiastic. Danger signal. Fear. A consuming passion--either negative or positive. Purification.

Fireman--Authority figure. Protector. One who may solve problems.

Fish--Emotional problems; indecisions. Water symbol, sex. Freudian phallic symbol. Christian symbol for spirituality; Jesus, fisher of men. (American Indian: A colorful fish with long, luxurious fins may represent a person concerned too much with the "frills" of life to be a trusted friend.)

Floating--Carefree. Freudian wish fulfillment to return to the womb. Astral travel. Peace.

Flowers--Love. Happiness. Marriage. Peace. Funeral.

Flying--Jungian: flying above earthly problems. Overcoming. Carefree. Freudian: sexual activity. Astral travel. Emotional evaluation.

Fog--Emotional. Not sure of course to follow.

Food--Love symbol. Nourishment of mind, body, spirit.

Foreigner--Something foreign to your own nature, unusual, odd. Feeling of being a stranger. Insecurity.

Fountain--Spiritual. Inner energy or love. Sex symbol.

Funeral--Death of ideas or a change in your thinking. Sometimes denotes a breaking away from negative thinking.

Furs--A wish for wealth.

Giant--Threatening people or conditions. Strength without wisdom.

Glacier or *Iceberg*--Sign of frigidity; cold feeling toward others. A danger that is largely hidden from view.

Glass--If through a window: looking for future. If glass is dirty: uncertainty about future.

Gloves--Denotes need for using care in certain situations. Protection.

Goat--Use caution. Do not turn your back on this situation. Pan, the power in nature. Vigorous sexual activity.

Goblin--Uncertainty. Fear.

God--This, of course, depends on your concept of God. Higher Self. What attributes do you associate with God (love, peace, harmony, jealousy, fear, etc.)?

Gold--Love. Wealth. A goal to be reached.

Goldfish--Inactivity. Aimlessness.

Gorilla--Father symbol (Freudian). Power. Threat.

Graduating from School--Spiritual symbol for an initiation. Reaching a goal. Success.

Grail, Holy--A search for God or Higher Self.

Grandfather--The Higher Self. Wisdom. Wise council. Teacher.

Grandmother--The Higher Self. Comfort. Love. Wisdom. Teacher.

Grapes--Spiritual food. An escape from reality. Sexual freedom. Sensuality. Comfort. Plenty.

Grass--Fertility symbol. Marriage hope. Peaceful surroundings.

Grave--Lost hopes. End of plans. A change.

Grief--Reflection of conscious conditions. Sometimes associated with death wish for another.

Guardian--The Higher Self. Spirit Guide. Guardian angel.

Guillotine--Freudian symbol for castration. Warning not to "lose your head" in a matter. Possible reincarnation dream of past life.

Gun--Possible hostility. Fear. Freudian sex symbol; phallic. Self-defense.

Gutter--Low state of thinking. Immorality. Rejection. Giving up hope.

Gypsy--Gaiety. Love. Restlessness. Uncertainty. Eat, drink, and be merry. Passion. Sex. Money. Freedom. Mystery.

Hair--If *soft and clean*: spiritual beauty; if *matted and dirty*: spiritually unclean; if *thinning or bald*: a man may feel consciousness of his age, or of aging. Seeing another as he really is. Gray or white represents wisdom. A haircut may represent loss of vitality.

Hand--Washing means spiritual cleansing or withdrawing from a situation. The right hand represents the conscious mind, while the left hand is the subconscious.

Harem--Emotional or sexual insecurity. The many facets of a woman's life. Variety.

Harp--Depending on your religious background, it could represent higher consciousness. Concealed death wish.

Harvest--A time for reaping life's rewards, spiritual or financial.

Hat--Power. Wisdom. Freudian: female symbol. Protection.

Hawk--Benevolence. A person with a strong desire to be useful and to help others (American Indian medicine symbol).

Head--Similar to Hat. Center of wisdom, power, etc.

Heart--Center of love.

Heart attack--Often precludes a romance (an attack of the heart). Seldom related to physical heart attack.

Heaven--Peace, fulfillment, and happiness. Reward.

Hell--Hidden guilt feelings. Depression. Hopelessness.

High School--The higher school of life. Purpose. Need to learn spiritual lessons.

Highway--May be admonishment to take the "high" way instead of the "low" way. Desire for travel. Trying to escape problems --the highway leaving town, etc.

Hill--A slight obstacle to overcome. A problem. Security from outside sources if several hills form a valley.

Hog or *Pig*--Greediness to be overcome. Unfair authority. Desire to be less inhibited.

Home--Your true home, spiritually. Family. Friends. Warmth. Comfort. Security. One's state of consciousness. The personality.

Honey--Pleasant things. Love. Sex. Spiritual food.

Horse--Beauty. Power. Messenger. Carrier. A lame horse may denote sickness. Passion, if horse is rearing or wild. Romance. (American Indian medicine symbol: An honest worker. A faithful, strong and healthy person.)

Hospital--Confinement. A need to consider health. A need for love or fulfillment. A need for attention.

House--The body of the dreamer. *Basement*: subconscious. *Attic*: mind. Empty rooms need to be filled spiritually. *Kitchen*: watch your diet. If the house is neat, chances are your life is orderly. If cluttered, time for setting the house in order.

Hunger--Emotional or spiritual need. Dissatisfaction.

Ice--Frigidity. Skating on thin ice: danger signal; breaking the ice: new friendship.

Ice Cream--Friendship, love, especially in children's dreams.

Idiot--Irresponsibility. Foolish ideas. Seeing yourself as such.

Idol--Worshipping false idols, "gods," such as money. Placing someone on a pedestal.

Illness--Escape from everyday problems of life.

India--A search for the mystical. Possible past-life recall.

Inheritance--Gain. Desire for wealth. Spiritual inheritance.

Invasion--Invasion of one's privacy or inner thoughts. Secrets revealed. Rape fear.

Ironing--To straighten or iron out one's problems.

Island--Seclusion. Desire to get away from it all. Security. A place of few inhibitions.

Ivory--Ivory palaces denote wealth. Spiritual attainment. High ideals.

Jail--Imprisoned by life's problems. Feeling of being walled in.

Jailer--Authority figure. Someone responsible for your problems.

Janitor--Hard work cleaning up your problems. Looking both ways (Janus, Latin god) as an impartial viewer of a problem.

Jealousy--Usually literal, reflecting conscious nature of the dreamer.

Jesus--Desire to reach higher spiritual perfection.

Jewels--Desire for wealth. Freudian sensual feeling if jewels are hidden.

Joan of Arc--A common symbol denoting courage or valor.

Job (biblical character)--The overcoming of earlier problems. In a quandary. To be tormented in a matter you consider unjust.

Journey, Travel--Normal to those who travel much in their work, but to nontravelers it can indicate a substitute word for "death."

Judge--Authority figure. One who views objectively and fairly. Superego. Need for Self-discipline. Hidden guilt.

Jury--Feeling that you are being judged by your friends or peers. Guilt feeling.

Key--The answer to a problem. Opening new doorways of opportunity. Gaining of new knowledge or wisdom. Providing safety.

Kill or *Killing*--Need to "kill" some negative aspect of your life.

King or *Queen*--Authority figure. One's father, or mother, boss or other in authority over you. Beneficent or demonic, depending on how you view this authority figure.

Kiss--A love symbol that is rather obvious. "Kiss of death"; betrayal.

Kitchen--A warning not to overeat. Watch your diet. A place of love, warmth, and friendship. Health.

Knife--Another Freudian phallic symbol. To be betrayed or to betray another; the "knife in the back" concept. Also symbol to cut out a bad habit. Sometimes the death wish for another or Self.

Knight--Bravery; valor. Authority figure. Hero. Desire for romance.

Laboratory--A place of harmonious blending. Seeking answers to problems. The mind.

Ladder--The spiritual climb to higher levels. Beware of a fall.

Lake--Water symbol for spirit. Peace if placid or smooth; turmoil if rough. Freudian symbol for desire for safety by returning to the womb.

Lamb--The Lamb of God. Gentleness. Sacrifice.

Lame--You are not fully understood. A mental or emotional hurt. Psychological cripple.

Lamp--Spiritual light. A showing of the Way. Knowledge and Wisdom.

Landlord, Landlady--Authority figure. Prestige, wealth, influence.

Late, Tardy--Overcommitted. Not achieving what you want in life. Desire to avoid certain things. You may be nearly too late to gain certain important goals.

Laughing--Sometimes literal, if the dream is humorous, but can also be mirror dream, crying. If someone is laughing at you, not with you, it may denote hypocritical tendencies on your part. You are not what you want others to believe you are.

Laundry--A need for spiritual or physical cleansing.

Law--Refers to Karmic Law. Law of life.

Lawn--If green: life is fulfilling; if brown: barren.

Leech--Someone may be draining you spiritually and emotionally.

Leopard--Cunning, skill, or treachery.

Letter--Good news. A desired message. If the letter is from someone specific, you may be about to hear from an old friend.

Light--Enlightenment. Pay attention to that to which the light directs you. Out of the darkness.

Lily--Spiritual symbol for purity. May mean a loss. Funeral or death of loved one.

Lion--Courage. Prowess. Power. Regal splendor. Royalty. Ambition.

Lock--Emotionally locked up. Locking others out of your life, or feeling you are locked out of theirs.

Locomotive--Drive, determination.

Losing Something--The loss of an object sometimes reflects sadness at the loss of a loved one or friend.

Luggage--Desire to travel. Prestige. Burdens, physical or psychological, that you carry with you.

Mad Person (insane)--Unacceptable feelings. Wild ideas, senseless.

Mansion--Desire for wealth, prestige. Past-life recall.

Marble--An enduring thing. Ancient concepts. Beauty. Cold, austere.

Marriage--Union, creativity, duty. Commitment. Initiation.
Meadow--If green: probably refers to a happy association; if brown: a loss.

Meat--Love. Brotherhood. Good companions. Cutting meat: possible increase; cooking meat: possible change; spoiled meat: danger.

Medicine--Need for medical attention.

Mending--Time to put your house in order. Corrective action needed. Improve relationships with others.

Merry-go-round--Going around in circles. Indecisions. Wish to return to carefree days of childhood. Desire to shed responsibilities.

Messenger--Higher Self.

Microscope--Finding a hidden meaning, a thing normally hard to see.

Milk--Love, particularly mother love. Spilled milk: your grasp is greater than your reach; sour milk: something has gone bad.

Minister--Superconscious guidance; authority figure. Need for solace.

Missing a Plane, Train, Boat, etc.--Life is passing you by. You have just missed attaining a very important goal.

Mirror--Sometimes reveals images of past life. Other times reveals one's true Self--good, bad, or indifferent. A reflection of the truth. How *others* see you. Can also represent *maya* , illusion, that which is not real, only a reflection.

Miser--To dream of a miserly person denotes that you may be withholding love and affection from another. A need to be more outgoing.

Money--Dreaming of wealth usually indicates achieving happiness in love. Finding money, finding love. Loss of money can indicate a loss of love or spiritual values. It also can literally indicate a desire for wealth.

Monkey--Are you making a fool (monkey) of yourself? Freudian symbol for sex fear in women; phallic symbol. A trickster. Instinctive energy.

Monk--Loyalty to one's religious beliefs, the Inner or Outer church. Dedication. Seclusion. Need for retreat.

Monument--Putting another on a pedestal.

Morning, Dawn--Conditions are getting better. Early, happy years of life. It can refer to "mourning" in the case of a lost loved one.

Mother--Authority figure. Unselfish love.

Mountain--Large problems in our lives. Obstacles to overcome. Spiritual goals. Attainment. (American Indian medicine symbol: Lofty ideals on two levels of awareness. If clouds surround the mountains, certain ideals may not be on a permanent foundation.)

Mouse--A potential to expand your awareness. Time to get into things that have been unused. Time to make better use of possessions or ideas that have been stored away (American Indian medicine symbol).

Movies or *Movie Stars*--Some aspect of your own life or personality. Relating to that actor or actress or scene. Mass consciousness or attitudes.

Moving--New conditions in your life are approaching. A desire to change a situation by starting over.

Mud, Muddy Water--Confusion; turmoil. A veil that separates the physical plane from the spiritual plane.
Murder--May signify hostility. Killing old ideas.

Nakedness--Seeing ourselves or others as we really are. Humility. Nothing to hide. Vulnerability.

Napoleon--Pretense. Unreasonable ambition. Trying to be something you are not. Also symbolic of power and accomplishment.

Necklace--Love or status.

Necktie--Bonds or ties in life.

Needle--Sewing indicates repairing errors of the past or may be someone giving you the "needle."

Neighbor--One who understands your problems. One experiencing problems similar to yours.

Nest--Childhood home.

Newspaper--New situations. Current events. Public attention.

Night, Darkness--Symbolic of old age or fear of growing old. Loneliness. Lacking understanding--in the dark about the problem at hand.

Noon--High point of activity. Busy.

Nurse--Mother symbol. A need for attention. An approaching illness.

Oak Tree--Father image. Oak worshipping in antiquity. Long life. Endurance. Strength.

Oar, Oarsman--The struggle of life. A crossing over from physical to spiritual realities.

Ocean--Spirit, God, Higher Self. Peace, unless a rough sea, then turmoil, strife, etc.

Orange Blossoms--Subconscious association with weddings.

Oranges--Purity. Awareness. Good health.

Orchestra--Forces in your life that may be in or out of harmony.

Organ Music--Love. Freudian concept: sex. Jungian: religious significance.

Ostrich--Desire to hide from your problems.

Overcoat--Desire to "cover up" a situation. Love. Protection.

Owl-Symbol of wisdom. Wise decision. Admonishment to think through a problem before making a decision.

Oyster--Secretive nature. Hidden wealth (pearl).

Painting or *Drawing*--Desire to be more creative.

Palace or *Castle*--Searching for the many rooms of your spiritual Self.

Parade--Life's past events on parade. Contemplating the many roles you play in this life, as well as others, as the characters in the parade generally are facets of your own Self.

Paralyzed--This dream often means you feel unable to cope with a problem. Fear of a situation.

Parents--Those who are available to assist you.

Partner--This can represent one's alter ego, helpmate or marriage partner.

Passenger--Are you letting someone else do the driving in your life? Does someone else make your major decisions?

Pawnshop--Money problems evident in past, present, or future. Warning to be careful in matters of finance.

Peacock--Undue pride. False pride.

Pen or *Pencil*--Desire to communicate thoughts to others. A wish for better understanding.

Pennies--Like money, a love symbol. Are you being shortchanged?

Pennies instead of dollars?

People, Crowds--Like a parade, often facets of your own personality or past-life personalities in review. Freudian symbol for secrecy, especially personal secret. Fear of someone learning your secrets.

Pig--Selfishness.

Plaintiff--Authority figure if you are the defender. Do you needlessly blame others; are you the plaintiff?

Platform, Stage--Do you feel you are above others? Elevation.

Policeman--Authority figure. Protection. Signal to slow down your activities. Conscience. Bring disorder under control.

Postman--Message.

President--Authority figure. Main person or aspect of your life.

Price Tag--Are you paying too much for something in time, energy, or money?

Priest--Superconscious guidance. Need for spiritual examination.

Prince or *Princess*--Desires.

Prostitute--Are you "prostituting" your abilities and talents? Can literally serve as a warning against immoral acts.

Purse--Freudian sex symbol. New opportunities. Money about to enter your life.

Pyramid--Initiation. Rising of spiritual power.

Quarrel--Literal relation to present problems. A disguise for love.

Quilt--To cover a problem. Confusion. Symbol of love, protection, warmth.

Rabbi--Superconscious guidance. Spiritual attunement.

Rabbit--Timidity; pity for another. Increase. (American Indian medicine symbol: A person who is always ready to handle challenges, but sometimes acts prematurely.)

Race, Racing--Ambition, desire for success. Winning the race; success.

Radio--Learning something from a distant source. Your capacity to "tune in" to yourself or others.

Rags--Despair. Mental or emotional poverty. Need for spiritual uplift, spiritual wealth.

Railroad Train--Desire to travel. Avoiding current problems. Escape. Review of your journey through life.

Rain--Blessings, benefits. Nurturance. Sadness. Release of emotions. A need to drink more wisdom.

Rainbow--Hope. Peace. Spiritual fulfillment.

Rake--Gathering in hope or problems; needed spiritual cleansing.

Rape--Avoid carelessness. Watch your behavior and your companions.

Rat--Filth, debris, disease.

Raven--Regret. Despair. Do not live in the past.

Reaching--Anxiety. Reaching for unrealistic goals.

Reading--A desire for further knowledge or enlightenment.

Rear, Looking to--Living in the past. Profit by past errors.

Records--Are you reviewing your past life or Akashic Record? Listening to old records may indicate a desire for the "good old days." Nostalgia.

Red Hair--Vitality, temper, psychic ability, energy.

Reducing--If not literal admonishment, can denote the loss of friendship. Loss of respect for another or Self.

Rehearsal--Unless you are an actor or actress, may denote planning or getting ready for an event.

Rejuvenate--Hope. Happiness. Promise of a better future.

Relatives--May indicate astral travel to loved ones on this plane or other planes of existence if they are deceased. Relatives also often represent parts of the dreamer's Self playing various roles of his life.

Repairing Something--Making amends for something you have done.

Restaurant--May refer to emotional or spiritual hunger that needs fulfilling.

Reunion--May be gathering with loved ones on higher planes. Gathering of ideas. Unifying one's thoughts.
Revelation--Literally may be a revelatory experience. A teaching dream. New facts to be presented.

Revival--Renewed energy. Upliftment.

Revolver, Hand Gun, Pistol--Freudian sex fear. Anger. Hostility. Admonishment to "improve your aim in life."

Rice--Wedding.

Ring--Eternity. Devotion. Love. Attunement.

Ringing Bell--Someone is trying to get your attention.

River--Barrier. Time. Peace. Way of life. Energy. Passage of time. Source of fertility.

Rocks--Wealth. Diamonds. Money. Life's rocky path. Strength. Stability. "Stoney" or cold.

Rooms--Various parts of one's Self.

Rosary--Repentance. Spiritual lessons.

Roundup--Gathering of ideas. Going along with the crowd.

Ruins--Emotional problems. Despair.

Running--Escaping a problem.

Rustic Setting--Peace or desire for solitude.

Sailor--Adventure. Love for travel and the sea. Courage.

Salad--Vitality. A need to mix with others.

Salt--Something of great value. Death of ideas.

Scales--Justice. Weighing values.

Scar--A hurt from the past. Healing.

School--Symbol for school of life. Lessons on Earth.

Scream--Fear. Calling attention to a problem.

Screen--Separating the chaff from the grain.

Scythe--Ending a situation. The Reaper with the scythe is, of course, the death symbol, but usually in a dream it denotes the death of old ways.

Seagull--A coming voyage. A high-flying seagull represents the expression of inner knowing and feelings of Self-satisfaction.

Searchlight--Shedding light on new ideas or spiritual values.

Secretary--Help needed with a problem. Confidential associate. Helpmate. A need to "record," to take notice of something.

Seed--Life begets life. New beginnings. Offspring. Word of Truth. Fertility. Planting an idea. Faith (mustard seed).

Sentry--Guarding one's secrets. Admonishment to keep a watch on someone or something.

Sewing--Creating new things or thoughts. Marriage. Domestic happiness. Also repairing "torn" friendship.

Sex--Integration. Union. Aggression.

Shadow--Protection. Mystery. Dark aspects of life.

Shampooing Hair--Spiritual cleansing.

Shark--Beware of unscrupulous individuals (loan sharks, etc.).

Sheep--Timidity.

Sheet--Covering something up. Blank.

Shelf or *Pigeonhole*--The place for something not understood, but not rejected. Storing knowledge for the future.

Shoes--Desire to make a move; travel. Old, worn out; depression.

Your foundation. Your basic principles.

Shower--Good fortune. New Hope. New Life. Spiritual cleansing.

Silver--Spiritual value.

Singing--Happiness. Love. Exultation.

Skating, Ice--Caution; some risk in your current venture.

Skeleton--Death fear symbol. Stripping way of all pretense.

Slap or Slapping--Being slapped: disapproving the actions of another person. An insult.

Slave--Is there a past situation that you have not released so that you might grow toward greater freedom?

Sleep--Dreaming of being asleep generally indicates a problem of which we are not fully aware.

Slip--Wearing a slip is sometimes the subconscious telling you of a slip or mistake you have made.

Slot Machines (and other gambling devices)--Warning against gambling too heavily on a business venture or personal investment.

Smoke--Danger signal. Problem brewing.

Snail--Sticking steadfastly to a routine. A creative idea that will come to fruition (American Indian medicine symbol).

Snake--Sex symbol (Freudian). Wisdom. Enemy. (American Indian: A person who has the ability to develop his or her inner-knowing and wisdom.) Temptation. Kundalini--pure, creative energy. The paradoxes of good/evil and wisdom/temptation.

Snow--Frigidity. Purity. Peace. Death. Chilling one's emotions toward someone.

Soap--Spiritual cleansing. Washing away problems.

Soldier--Protection. Bravery. To the ex-GI it may mean a desire to return to the comradeship of the service, or to that life where someone else does most of your thinking for you.

Solomon--Wisdom. Wise decision.

Son--For a man, the younger Self or responsibilities.

South--Warmth. Carefree vacation from life's problems. Happiness. Dreaming of going north may have opposite meaning.

Spectacles (glasses)--A need to better understand (see) a problem.

Spider--Distrust. Fear. Orderliness. Beauty. Depends on your personal feelings toward spiders.

Sponge--There is someone who takes advantage of you. Warning that you may be taking advantage of another person.

Spring--Eternal youth. Happiness. Joy. Renewed life.

Square--Things in balance. Fullness. Completeness.

Star of David--Prophecy. Spiritual illumination.

Stars--Reaching for the higher spiritual values.

Starvation--Emotional hunger.

Steps--Upward climb spiritually.

Stocks and Bonds--Fluctuating trends in one's life.

Storm--Turmoil in life. Problems.

Stove, Oven--Warmth, love, and comfort.

Street--Your spiritual path.

String--Something that binds things together. Your link to others.

Student--A student in the School of Life. Spiritual studies.

Submarine--The subconscious.

Subway--Subconscious.

Suit--A new suit may signify a new outlook or way of life; an old suit may signify a need for change.

Suitcase, Luggage--Prosperity. Desire to travel. Prestige. Subconscious desire for someone else to go away.

Summer--Happiness, joy, warmth.

Sun--Spiritual light and awareness.

Sunset--The happy ending to a situation. Peace.

Swamp--Confusion. Overwork. Fear of something. Need for more spiritual enlightenment.

Swan--The spirit. Pride. Solitary grace.

Swimming--At ease with the subconscious.

Sword--Power. Honor. Authority. War. Protection. Strength of character. Freudian phallic symbol.

Tablet, paper--A message from the subconscious.

Tablet, stone--A message from the superconscious.

Talmud---Spiritual wisdom.

Tapestry--Wealth. Oriental wisdom. Royalty.

Teacher--If not a teaching dream, authority figure. Need for learning certain lessons. Admonishment to study harder.

Tear--A torn relationship.

Teeth--The loss of a tooth or teeth may foretell the loss of something of value. Fear of old age. Actual need for dental work. The spoken word.

Telegram--Often foretells of a coming message. Urgency.

Telephone--Common in telepathic dreams, since we can readily identify with a telephone, but not always with telepathy itself. Inner messages.

Temper--Freudian disguises for love. Same as in conscious state, emotional release.

Temple--Assistance in understanding spiritual welfare.

Tenement Building--Shabby conditions. Time to put your house in order.

Test--Are you ready to advance spiritually or in business?

Thanksgiving--Happiness. Plenty. Prosperity. Thankfulness. A time of coming together in understanding with relatives or friends.

Theater--You are on the stage of life, or as Shakespeare said, we are all actors on the stage of life, making our entrances, reading our lines and making our exits.

Thief--Someone who steals from you emotionally or spiritually. Time thief.

Thinness--Emotional starvation.

Throne--Do you place someone else on a throne or pedestal? Are you on an ego trip?

Tie--Emotional ties.

Tip (gratuity)--Reward for something well done.

Toboggan, Sled--Are you going downhill morally or physically? A return to the more pleasant "ups and downs" of childhood.

Toilet--Emotional, spiritual, or psychological cleansing is taking place or is needed.

Top or *Apex*--Reaching a goal.

Toys--Toying with ideas.

Trash Pile--Discarding unworthy ideas or thoughts.

Tree--Life. The kind of tree may denote the kind of life. The oak is solid; the willow is wispy; the poplar is graceful, etc. Aspiration. Development. Fruitfulness.

Triangle--Usually refers to the love triangle, but also may have deeper esoteric meanings.

Tricycle--Childishness. May be similar to triangle.

Truck--Are you carrying heavy burdens?

Turtle--Slow but steady is often the best policy. Strength. (American Indian: A symbol of peace. A person who may be misunderstood because of his or her determination and stubbornness.)

Umbrella--Shielding from or by something. Emotional safeguard.

Undressing--Indicates the dreamer is not trying to hide anything.

Veil--Marriage. Hiding something. Secrets.

Waiter or *Waitress*--Service to others (if you are the waiter or waitress) or expecting others to serve you.

Wall--Obstacles. Keeping to one's Self. Protection.

Wallet--Wealth. Position.

War--Conflicting ideas.

Washing--Spiritual cleansing.

Watch--It may be later than you think. Caution. Be watchful.

Water--Source of Life. Spirit, God, Universal Intelligence. Creativity. Troubled waters: problem; calm waters: peace, harmony.

Wave--Conditions are unstable.

Weakness--Seeing weakness or physical impairment in others often refers to problems within ourselves. A blind person might, for example, mean the dreamer is "blind" to a certain condition or problem. A cripple might tell the dreamer he is not walking in balance, etc.

Wedding--Sometimes prophetic. Mirrored meaning might indicate a forthcoming death. A joining of forces or ideas. Happiness.

Weeds--Neglect. Something choking out good or growth.

West--This is a symbol that has sometimes meant death--heading into the sunset of life. Can also mean wealth, as related to gold rushes in the West. Opportunity.

Whale--A problem. Ancient concept; i.e., "Jonah and the whale" when he was in a quandary. Symbol of protective influence.

Whispering--Secretive. Surprise.

Widow, Widower--A loss of a partner, business or real estate. Beginning a new life.

Witch (fairytale variety)--Mystery; intrigue. Supernatural. Disenchantment.

Wizard--Hidden force.

Wolf--Financial problems.

Wound--Emotional hurt.

Wrestling--Emotional turmoil. Wrestling with a problem.

X-ray--To see through something or someone.

Yardstick--A measure of one's success or failure.

Youth--It is not uncommon to dream of ourselves in eternal youth, since the Self is eternally young.